CITY SHADOWS

Dr Arnold Mindell

CITY SHADOWS
Psychological Interventions
in Psychiatry

R

Routledge
London & New York

First published in 1988 by
Routledge
11 New Fetter Lane, London EC4P 4EE

Published in the USA by
Routledge
a division of Routledge, Chapman and Hall, Inc.
29 West 35th Street, New York, NY 10001

Set in 10/12pt. Palatino
by Columns of Reading
and printed in the British Isles
by The Guernsey Press Co Ltd.
Guernsey Channel Islands

Library of Congress Cataloging in Publication Data
Mindell, Arnold, 1940–
  City shadows.
  Includes index.
  1. Psychiatry.   I. Title.   [DNIM: 1. Mental Disorders
  —therapy.   2. Psychology, Applied.   WM 400 M663c]
  RC454.4.6   1988   616.89   87-32196

British Library Cataloguing in Publication Data
Mindell, Arnold
  City shadows : psychological interventions
  in psychiatry.
  1. Psychiatry
  I. Title
  616.89   RC454

ISBN 0-415-00193-5

To Dieter Wartenweiler

CONTENTS

ACKNOWLEDGMENTS

I am indebted to several Swiss Social Service centers for exciting supervision weeks from which many of the reports presented in this text are derived. Only the names and personal material of the people we worked with during those weeks have been changed in the otherwise verbatim transcripts of video tapes.

I am also greatly indebted to Dr Dieter Wartenweiler for having inspired me to do this work. I am also thankful to Dr Joe Goodbread, Jean Claude Audergon, Ursula Hohler and Dr Kathy Ziegler for participating with me, holding my hand and helping me prepare some of the methods for the interactions which occurred during those weeks. I am particularly thankful to the 'Sozialdienst' of the City of Zurich and of Dubendorf for asking me to supervise their training programs. I gained much insight from these groups into the nature of social psychiatric problems, especially those dealing with criminal behavior.

Many special thanks to Amy Kaplan for numerous debates, clarifying discussions and supporting material, especially concerning the topics of Chapters 2, 3, 4 and 5. Ursula Hohler also helped me a great deal by commenting and adding to the original text. Special thanks go to Dr Samuel Wiener for his useful comments and criticisms of the manuscript. Furthermore, the following individuals have greatly improved this manuscript by offering their criticism, suggestions and information about psychiatric hospitals, conditions and language: Jim Beggs, Larry Bearg, Erwin

Lichtenegger, Jan Loeken, George Mecouch, Dawn Menken, Carl Mindell, Scott Sandage, Suzanne Springs, Dieter Wartenweiler, Kathy Ziegler, and Adam Zwig. I am especially grateful to Julie Diamond for her enthusiastic editorial help.

I am indebted to the students of my psychiatry class at the Research Society for Process Oriented Psychology in Zurich for going over the case material of this book with me as it was presented in lecture form. They challenged me to express unconscious beliefs, goals and speculations which otherwise would have remained unconscious.

And finally, I am immensely grateful to those many clients with whom I have worked during the last twenty-five years who have suffered through their extreme and border-line states with me and showed me clearly where my inner representation of their realities had been incomplete. In the final evaluation, they have turned out to be my most important teachers about psychotic phenomena.

For general information about Process Oriented Psychology, please write in the USA to:

Dr Suzanne Springs
Research Society for POP
PO Box 38572
Denver Co 80238

and in Europe to:

Madeleine Ziegler, Lic Phil
Research Society for POP
Etzelstr 10
8038 Zurich
Switzerland

PREFACE

This work stems from the need to express my experiences and theories derived from many thousands of hours of work with people in the midst of extreme states, such as those occurring during psychotic episodes, drugged and hypnotic conditions, violent convulsions, the pain of physical diseases, parapsychological excitement and the events surrounding death.

The verbatim reports of work with clients which appear in the book come from the meticulously transcribed video tapes of a supervision seminar at a state-subsidized social work center in Switzerland.

The project consisted of fourteen interviews with clients, considered by the social services to be their most difficult cases. The original purpose of the seminar was to supervise the work already going on there. My experience with other social work agencies indicates that the present collection of clients' material is representative of the kinds of difficulties which any city meets when dealing with social psychiatric problems, or alternatively, which any client in need of social aid has with any given city in the modern western world.

The positive reactions from both the staff and the clients to using the process oriented paradigm lessened the heavy and sometimes hopeless feeling commonly experienced by many mental health professionals working with difficult clients and encouraged me to prepare this manuscript for publication. This book attempts give the reader an overview of methods for working with many different types of altered and psychotic states. The disadvantage is that this horizontal study does not give a complete view of the multiple causes and developmental psychology of a particular client, as she changes over long periods of time. Such a vertical study would be a very different kind of book and one which is now being attempted by my colleagues.

This work is based upon the concepts developed in *The Dreambody, Working with the Dreaming Body, River's Way, The Dreambody in Relationships* and *Inner Dreambody Work*. Application of process theory to non-psychotic states can be seen in the film *Introduction to Process oriented Psychology* (Grey, 1987). My background is based upon my work as an analyst in Process Oriented and Jungian psychology, my early studies in physics, my research and practice of body work and knowledge of information theory. I have been in private practice for over twenty-four years, have worked with various clinics and supervised the therapy of hundreds of psychotic patients. I am especially interested in alchemy and Taoism, the belief and practice that nature, that is, spontaneous happenings, contains the wisdom of the right way to deal with life.

Despite the frequently spectacular results of process work there are reasons for scepticism about its application. There are several problems inhibiting satisfactory treatment for anyone in need of help from a city's mental hospital or social work center, problems which do not immediately appear on paper or which cannot always be easily discussed.

First of all, what you are about to read is the result of twenty years of study and experience. It cannot be applied as easily as it appears on paper. To be able to do process work, the student of psychology, psychiatry, social work and medicine must not only be knowledgeable of his or her given profession but must also be trained in the perception, differentiation and methods of working with verbal and non-verbal signals. Some students are able to acquire this sort of training and education in a couple of years, most need five years of experience working with the methods of the process oriented paradigm to be able to deal with extreme states. How we process what we perceive is a deep and complicated matter involving our personal and collective psychology. Readers requiring further background in process oriented signal studies can find this in my *Working with the Dreaming Body* and *River's Way*.

The second problem which arises in applying the process oriented paradigm is having to shift from the medical model which attempts to determine and ameliorate causes of phenomena to a model which creates change through appreciating what is happening. Such a change is bound to arouse resistance in professionals who are already firmly established in their policies and methods of treatment. I find this resistance a welcome and exciting challenge, for, when used constructively, it tests new ideas by pressing them to develop more fully.

Thus, I warmly invite any reactions from my readers and hope that those who find the following material difficult or irritating for one reason or another will share their insights and understanding so that I may learn how to better refine, teach and write about process concepts.

All of us involved in the mental health professions are, it seems to me, faced with many extreme situations which we feel we do not deal with satisfactorily. Though we can quiet down our most difficult clients, control extreme cases, even ameliorate syndromes, we rarely feel that we have a model or a paradigm which is sufficient for handling the total personality and environment surrounding a psychotic episode or an individual who has become, for one reason or another, a permanent client of our hospitals and social work agencies. As a result, most therapists, analysts, psychiatrists and psychologists in private practice try to avoid extreme and borderline patients. I hope to show that we need to work together to discover the common thread in the most useful elements of our theories and practice.

Not only are there difficulties involved in the training and application of new ideas in psychology and psychiatry, but working with clients in a process oriented way entertains the philosophical concept that these clients might be meaningful for the city they live in. Such concepts are not always greeted enthusiastically by city officials. Like any family housing an 'identified patient,' the city itself resists and will continue to resist the idea that it, too, may have to change if its 'patients' are to get better. The city's attitude is understandable, yet it ignores any potential responsibility it may have in generating the difficulties in its communal family.

Thus the original optimism and simplicity which appears in the following pages should be tempered by knowledge of the complex nature of the network changes involved in any one particular case confronting a social agency. The satisfactory treatment of the individual client in the midst of extreme states involves not only the psychology of his helper and the science of extreme states, but also the psychology of the entire city, state and world in which he lives.

My advice is to bring up these problems, spell them out and not be naïve about them. Working with troubled people has unavoidable political implications. The process of a single person in need of aid from a city hospital, out-patient clinic, social work center or police department implies change in the client, greater research into altered states of consciousness, changes in the special training of the mental health professional to deal with his or her internal problems and with the agency, changes in the attitude of city officials and interactions with the public.

May the following manuscript be a hint about how to meet at least the client's part of the immense network of difficulties surrounding the highly unusual client, the therapist, the agency to which this therapist belongs and the city in which the client lives.

Part 1
INTRODUCTION

Chapter I
PSYCHIATRY IN CRISIS

This book is written for both students and experienced professionals, psychiatrists, psychologists, psychiatric social workers, nurses, nurses' aides, secretaries, city officials, interested laymen and family members, who, by profession or out of compassion, must deal with the wide spectrum of people who are dependent upon the city's social work agencies, drug rehabilitation centers or mental hospitals for financial, psychological and moral support. It is a work written in the spirit of new beginnings. What are the full implications of process work with extreme states?

At the present time, near the end of the 1980s, the most common paradigm in psychiatry is the so-called 'medical model.' This model has various aspects to it. At its core lies the concept of causality and the related programs of defining disease, searching for its causes and attempting to cure it with behavioral and chemical interventions. This program organizes definitions, research and treatments of what are defined mental illnesses.

The biomedical paradigm has proven to be useful in the cure and amelioration of symptoms in medicine and psychiatry, though its applicability to the latter is debated by many authors [Greist et al., 1982). The global, and by now common, critiques of modern psychiatry usually deal with the incongruity of its focus. If it deals mainly with mood states, with affects, feelings, hallucinations and disturbed belief systems, then, according to many, it should stand on its own relative to its parent, modern medicine, and not simply adapt medical concepts which only partly apply to non-physical disease descriptions.

CONTENTS OF THIS WORK

A process oriented approach which attempts to discover the structure and flow of 'psychotic' states is presented and compared to given medical techniques. Thus, the terms and diagnoses of the Diagnostic and Statistical Manual of Mental Disorders (DSM III 1980), the most accepted and clearly formulated medical statement about mental disorders, is related to and differentiated from process work throughout this text. (See the Glossary for the connection between psychiatric and process work terms.)

Verbatim interviews are transcribed from video tape recordings and psychotherapeutic interventions of disease entities such as schizophrenia, manic-depressive reactions (or bipolar disease), mania, depression, suicide, psychopathy, organic brain damage, alcoholism, heroin addiction, epilepsy, imbecility, forensic psychiatric problems and sociopathy are presented here.

The biomedical model and associated methods for dealing with the above mentioned classifications do not fully achieve their implicit or explicit healing goals (Boyle, and Morriss, Griest, et al., 1982; Torrey, 1974). However, this model manages most acute psychiatric problems and makes it possible for many to come through extreme states in relatively short periods of time. Since many aspects of the healing goal are not fulfilled, psychiatry might be termed, using T. Kuhn's analysis of scientific revolutions, 'a science in the midst of an evolutionary crisis' (Kuhn, 1970).

This chapter describes that crisis. The second chapter presents the theory of process work and is followed by descriptions and demonstrations of the process paradigm applied to cases of schizophrenia, mania, depression, drug dependency, psychopathy and related states. Finally, in the last chapter, the implications of studying extreme states upon psychiatry, psychology, social work and politics are discussed.

The belief governing this work is that integrating psychiatry with psychology will create important changes in both. It seems to me that extreme human states are to psychology what astronomical phenomena were to physics before Einstein's theory of relativity: namely, facts which do not fit present theories.

PARADIGMS AND INTERVENTIONS

A given paradigm determines the observational methods and treatments of the patients. Basic to medicine in all cultures, including ours, is the assumption that people who do not function in a given society are ill; they are not in order and require change. Thus, if we assume that people are sick, we shall find its cause and eradicate it. Our observations focus upon the symptoms which correspond to our definition of a given illness. Curing a patient means, then, eradicating his symptoms so that he corresponds to our definition of normalcy.

My conclusion from supervising psychiatrists and psychologists working with psychotic patients is that when the above paradigm does not produce the desired results, the reason for failure is not always due to a given therapist's inability to apply the medical model. A core difficulty in dealing with psychotic states is frequently traceable to insufficient training in observing the actual details of the patient's behavior. Thus, the detailed behavior of the individual patient is frequently glossed over. For example, a patient who is very passive and involved in his treatment is obviously going to be more responsive to medication than another patient who considers herself a revolutionary and finds it necessary to despise authority. In the process paradigm, to be presented briefly in the next chapter, the client is not considered, a priori, to be sick. We do not assume that his brain is functioning improperly, or that he is conscious or unconscious. Rather, the exact nature and content of his utterances and body signals are studied with the idea in mind that appreciating these details will help him best. We assume that if the signals and goals of altered and normal states are followed, life is going to be more worthwhile to him afterwards than if we only attempted to get him back on his feet and function again.

Process oriented psychology is a wide spectrum method of perceiving, differentiating and enabling human signals, both close to and far from the personal identity of the doctor and patient, to unfold. The aim of process oriented psychology is to allow these different signals and states to unfold in an individual way which depends upon the client and the therapist, by focusing on the underlying process structures which connect them. In fact, the most able therapist appears to be one who is familiar with all parts of psychology, including dream and body work, meditation, psychosomatic medicine, medical terminology and treatments, relationship and family work, social work, etc. An empirical discovery is that present problems and issues become their own solutions, their own 'cures,' if you will.

Though there are many indications that psychology and psychiatry might grow together, the mental health practitioner today generally uses pieces of different psychologies, medicines and psychiatry to help her clients. These various disciplines, based upon different and sometimes contradictory philosophies, have different methods of empirical investigation and treatment, yet they deal with one and the same person. Medicine attempts to enable patients to function like the rest of their environment. However, since medicine alone may not improve the quality of an individual's life, most therapists frequently add psychological interventions to their practice. Most psychologies today, however, are unable to deal with the gravity of psychiatric situations alone.

While such differences have the advantage of creating individual and global approaches to the human being, they could become even more valuable if the unitary background to the psychological sciences were better understood. A disadvantage to having several different paradigms of mental health is that the competition among them draws energy away from treating the client and may hinder the cooperation and team work necessary for creating a more functional approach to the individual suffering from extreme states.

THE CRISIS IN PSYCHIATRY
The situation in modern psychiatry is summed up by Freedman et al. (1980) in their *Modern Synopsis of Psychiatry/IV*. In the Preface it is stated

> Sometimes the structures (of American life) and groups cooperate, but often they act in competition with one another. Each has its own responsibilities, and the fulfillment of these responsibilities gives rise to diffuse goals. The operation of such groups is seldom conducive to the formation of unified conceptual systems, and the history of American psychiatric schools is no exception to this rule. This diversity is caused not only by the steady growth of knowledge within the United States but also the constant enrichment of American intellectual life through immigration. New ideas brought here by our colleagues from abroad have taken root and flourished. . . . To present this diversity in all of its richness and contradiction it is necessary to be truly eclectic. . . .
>   If pluralism is a feature of American life that demands recognition, then pragmatism is one which requires compensation. While truth needs testing by the practical consequences of belief, commonplace American pragmatism often goes beyond empiricism to a disregard for theory. Thus, American psychiatry has shown strength in the development of application of treatment methods while neglecting nosology and clinical description.

This picture of contemporary American psychiatry is, I believe, true of western psychiatry in general. The facts noted by Freedman et al. have certain implications:

1. *Psychiatry is a Pre-Science*
The eclectic state of affairs is an indication that a governing paradigm is missing in psychiatry and that both psychiatry and psychology are in a pre-scientific stage of development in the sense of having no single, generally accepted method or organization. This means that the mental health sciences

are governed in the moment, not only by experimental methods, but also by various beliefs and affects. Apparently there is no general agreement among psychiatrists at present about their identity or goals (Adler, 1981).

2. *Eclectic Pluralism Needs Processing*
The competition between the schools is correct and is something which requires processing. I can see a conference in which different approaches are presented and discussed. But discussion is not enough and it will become important to find some sort of unifying principle which ties together the various treatment methods. Then the school favoring the use of psychopharmica for psychotic states will, I believe, integrate what I shall call the 'meaning' schools of psychiatry. These schools favor behavioral and transpersonal paradigms, and perceive life from the viewpoint of peak religious experiences. Concepts such as antipsychiatry, social revolution, archetypal experiences, early split off childhood experiences, systemic structures and dysfunctional communication will then be differentiated into neutral concepts such as local and early causality, immediate environmental community effects and field influences from the entire planet.

3. *The Effect of Psychiatry's Problems on the Patient*
Present treatment methods which, as a general rule, are devoted to the individual patient are not only divided within themselves but are also frequently pitted against the city officials whose major interest is removing the 'disturbance' from the public eye. Thus, psychiatry is split within itself, divided from the various schools of psychology and frequently at odds with the city government, all of whom feel responsible in one way or another for the disturbed client. Under these circumstances, it is not surprising that the therapies for the individual are not as powerful as they could be, for their diversification frequently mirrors the compartmentalization characteristic of the disturbed person.

4. *Pragmatism is Still Incomplete*
The pragmatic attitude in psychiatry criticized by Freedman et al. has not gone far enough. The present medical cause and effect paradigm does not allow the mental health practitioner to observe phenomena from the viewpoint of the client. As a result, many definitions in psychiatry are based upon community platitudes and unconscious assumptions about normalcy. Thus, it is not surprising that treatment methods arising from these assumptions are not always effective.

5. *Iatrogenic Diseases*
Iatrogenic diseases are disorders caused by the medical profession itself. Today the medicines for many diseases create symptoms which are frequently only slightly preferable to those of the original disease. It is in fact common practice to accept drugs which ameliorate syndromes but which create new symptoms themselves.

One such occasionally occurring disorder, tardive dyskenisia (TD), may be mentioned. TD is a disorder arising in conjunction with many neuroleptic drugs which sometimes produce only marginal improvement of psychotic states. TD is potentially irreversible, involuntary or choreathoid movements which develop even after short term treatments (Kessler and Waletzky, 1981). Forty percent of elderly chronic patients now get it.

Even medical practitioners see some hallucinations as tolerable relative to the TD side effects (Janson et al., 1985). A recent report in *Psychiatric News* (May 17, 1986), lists several dozen drugs which carry TD side effects. These are Serentil, Moban, Innovar, Inapsine, Iositane, Haldol, Triovil, Taractarn, Navane, Mellarille, Thorazine, Sparine, etc.

6. *Problems in the Maintenance of the Chronically Ill*
Drugs, however, not only create other diseases, but seem to be erratic in dealing with relapses associated with highly emotional environments and difficult life situations. In

Introduction to Psychopharmacology (Lader, 1980, p. 58) we read that assessment studies on maintenance therapies (antipsychotic medication which suppresses chronic symptoms such as hallucinations) show that 'drugs made a demonstrable difference to patients in low EE homes.' An EE home is one where the closest relative at the time of the schizophrenic's admission was low on the number of critical, hostile or emotionally overcharged comments. 'Life events also seem important and tend to cluster in three weeks immediately before relapse.' Drug maintenance therapies seem relatively ineffective in preventing such event-related relapses, especially when life events are major.

There are other problems connected with medications besides their inefficiency. Many patients go off 'meds' not only because they found something of value in even the most nightmarish mental conditions, but also because they cannot tolerate either the drug's effects or the social implications of being drugged. These patients are disturbed about the overall effects drugs have or do not have on their lives.

7. *Psychiatry and Culture*
At present, psychiatric methods and theory support a basic cultural tendency: preserving the outer appearance of order while inhibiting direct experience of the psyche. As a result, the patient is seen as 'sick' and as a 'disturbance,' but not as the 'identified patient' of a community which itself needs to change if it expects the statistics of mental disorders to change.

8. *Lack of Theory in Psychiatry*
It is dangerous to outweigh the negative results of an experiment against the positive ones. In terms of antipsychotic drugs, it should be mentioned that the relatively recent explosion in research into the functioning of neuroleptica should be reason for optimism. This research creates the hope for many that biochemistry will solve the chemical problems behind mental disease in the future. Emotional support is given to this hope by the general ineffectiveness

of psychotherapies. There is a widespread agreement (Karon and Vandenbos, 1981, are exceptions) that psychoanalytic techniques, group therapy, analytical psychology and other psychotherapies do not work with psychotic situations (cf. Greist et al. 1982).

From a theoretical viewpoint, however, the inadequacies of both drugs and present psychotherapeutic techniques point not only to logical inconsistencies in the psychiatric viewpoint which lead to internal conflicts in that profession, but also to the fact that the governing, conflicting paradigms are insufficient to deal with the psychotic states they attempt to control. This means that the basis of psychiatry is in the midst of a revolution and points to an obvious conclusion. Let us begin again with basic principles and review our assumptions and methods.

The difficulty with such a beginner's mind approach to psychiatry is that clear perception requires new ways of thinking, new mind sets, so to speak. Emotionally, it is difficult for a practitioner who has studied until the age of thirty to begin at age fifty to review and speculate about the foundations of his work. This difficulty undoubtedly inhibits some professionals from thinking more deeply about their professions. Moreover, it is easier in many ways and perhaps less time consuming (to begin with at least) to describe disease characteristics and to recommend medicine for them than it is to determine, consider and probe the potential meaning and evolution of a psychotic process which so rambunctiously interrupts every normal state of communication and harmony.

PREDICTABILITY, ORDER AND DISORDER IN 'MENTAL ILLNESS'

Almost all psychiatric textbooks speak of mental diseases in terms of 'disintegration of the personality' and 'unbalanced and chaotic states.' Such descriptions are based upon the unexpressed assumption that the ideal person is able to correspond to the statistical average, and this average is taken as a measure of order, balance, harmony and health. Thus, it seems as if individuals going through psychotic states appear as the chaos and disorder for a culture with a particular idea of order and sanity. This black/white, polar classification of the human being lies at the root of DSM III, which only weakly tolerates the concept of a wellness-notwellness continuum of inner experiences. Change and differentiation are needed (cf. Boyle and Morriss; Engel, Greist et al., 1982).

Process concepts understand 'mental illness' as an extreme state which everyone goes through. As we shall see in the following chapters, process science perceives psychotic states not as chaotic, but as highly, even mathematically, ordered structures; they are not disintegrations, but highly patterned evolutions.

The concept of chaos and unpredictability is related to the therapist's or observer's awareness and experience. Predictability is a concept relative to a given observer and is not an absolute characteristic of a patient. As far as the therapist is concerned, what he sees in a client is a total surprise to him when information appears which he, the therapist, has never (consciously) been aware of before.

One of the tenets of process oriented psychology is that if you are surprised by someone, you have not consciously perceived signals forewarning you of a coming event. In other words, the 'chaos' or unpredictability of a client is a function of the therapist's inability to process information in front of him, not of the client's inherent 'disorder.' Suicide, insanity, unfaithfulness in relationships, criminal behavior, etc. are all apparent in the signal system of our clients and friends.

It is important for the therapist to constantly extend and improve his ability to pick up signals from his clients. We tend to focus only upon the content of what people say and do not pay conscious attention to their other signals, such as their tone of voice, their sitting position, the movement of their legs, etc.

EXTREME STATES
The more our perception improves, the less we will need to use terms such as 'disorder' and 'chaos.' In what follows, except where I need to differentiate process thinking from

medical paradigms, I shall refer to mental disorders as extreme states.

The word 'state' means for me a momentary picture of an evolving process. The term 'extreme' refers to the frequency with which these states are met with by the ordinary person during everyday conditions outside of the psychiatric milieu. Thus, they are rare only in terms of occurrence; the majority of their content and structure is experienced by all of us. In Chapters 4, 5 and 6 I will show that these extreme states show a chronically missing 'metacommunicator,' that is, someone who is able to talk about the states as if they were occurring in another person.

This definition of psychosis frees me to study these states as static momentary or cyclical processes which are evolving, have a purpose and an implicit order and direction. Furthermore, I am removing them from the ordinary categories of cause and effect, medical disease and cure, and placing them in the realm of phenomenology, which connects psychiatry to psychology, physics, medicine and sociology.

FREQUENCY OF OCCURRENCE AND TRANSCULTURAL PSYCHIATRY
The term 'extreme states' indicates a certain infrequency of occurrence for a given observer. A volcano for an inhabitant of Hawaii will not be an extreme condition, for a New Yorker or Zuricher, it will be. Hence, what is sick or extreme for one culture will not be for another. By using terms like 'extreme states' and 'process work,' we have the chance of developing a transcultural psychiatry which deals with relative deviations from the norm and which is independent of the specific cultural definitions of illness.

The western world differentiates its extreme states according to the way people in these states do or do not communicate. About one half of the people in our mental hospitals are said to suffer from what is diagnosed as schizophrenia, the rest are a mixture of severely depressed or suicidal people, the aged and senile, people in manic states, chronic alcoholics, heroin addicts, people with organic brain damage, the so-called criminally insane, those laboring under subnormal intelligence, and a large category entitled 'mixed psychoses,' those with a mixture of the above, or the 'generally handicapped.' These categories vary from one hospital and community to the next.

TREATMENT MODALITIES

It seems as if the newest treatment for psychiatric disorders will eventually be derived from computerized tomography (CT), an unobtrusive, acceptable radiologic view of the living brain which will probably increase the use of drugs in understanding the relationship between brain physiology and behavior. As yet, however, brain scan techniques have done more for stimulating brain-behavior research than for providing immediate practical applications (Serafetinides, 1985; Wyatt:1984).

The most popular treatment today for a given category is the administration of psychopharmica. Group therapy is probably the next most popular treatment of choice for city disturbers. Group therapy champions the integration of the client into the rest of the community. This form of therapy is linked with systems theory and family therapy, both of which work with the communication problems within the client's original milieu. The theory behind it is the assumption that the client's problems are supported indirectly by the world he comes from.

Neopsychoanalytic therapies seek an understanding relationship with the client, whom, it is hoped, will eventually achieve insight into his condition (Karon and Vandenbos, 1981). A Jungian development based upon empathetic understanding and patience is governed by the concept that the client is experiencing an archetypal drama which needs appreciation and understanding (Perry, 1974). More recent therapies such as dance therapy are aimed at enabling the client to express his condition more completely (Marion Chace, 1975; Schoop and Mitchell, 1974).

Transpersonal psychology is attempting to understand mental problems from a developmental viewpoint in which the human being is conceived as being en route to something like an Atman experience (Wilbur, 1984). No specific treatment is associated, as far as I know, with transpersonal psychology besides an appreciation of the meaning and significance of the disorder.

Jung assumed in the first part of this century that mental disturbances were not merely pathological but were manifestations of some meaningful behavior which he wanted to understand. He later amplified this theory by suspecting there to be chemical disturbance in schizophrenia (Jung, 1974).

In his autobiography, he tells about a schizophrenic woman who showed him that mental disease could be teleological. During his early work in Burgholzli, he examined an old woman suffering from schizophrenia and found that she continuously made the motions of a shoe maker. He discovered that just before she had lost her mind, a shoemaker had rejected her love, apparently precipitating the psychosis.

He tells of another catatonic woman who fantasized about living on the moon. Jung showed her that she had to live in this reality and that this was not going to be easy. He worked with another advanced schizophrenic woman who had voices coming out of her entire body. He listened to the ones which called themselves God coming from her thorax, followed their directions, gave her bible readings and she slowly improved. In time, this woman was freed from the voices coming from at least one-half of her body. Jung believed that when attending to the mentally ill one must be content with small improvements.

ANTI-PSYCHIATRY

I do not intend to give a history of psychiatry here, though such a study of the development of psychology would prove fascinating. Thus, I cannot do justice to the main forms of therapy, especially the popular behavioral treatments which reward the patient for changes in behavior. I must, however, mention the work of R.D. Laing, who, under the controlled conditions of a mental hospital, allows the 'schizophrenic' to let his process unfold. In some of Laing's writings, we begin to see the schizophrenic not as mad, but as a political radical relative to the world he lives in (Laing, 1967). Laing is easiest to read if we simultaneously consider the fact that he is compensating a world which fears the public consequences of madness.

CONCLUSION ABOUT THE CRISIS IN PSYCHIATRY

DSM III is a major step in the delineation of mental disorder. It also creates the impetus to unify the language and concepts of psychiatry in perhaps the most significant way since its beginning. Nevertheless, the lack of agreement over the identity of psychiatry relative to the rest of medicine, the relatively high frequency and seriousness of the iatrogenic diseases associated with neuroleptica, and the inefficiency of these drugs at the present time give room for reconsidering the foundations of work with extreme and psychotic states.

Furthermore, one of the basic assumptions of psychiatry, that disease entities are 'caused' by specific chemical imbalances, has not, until present, been verifiable. For example, schizophrenia strikes 1 percent of the population today, a percentage which has not decreased throughout history, in part because the supposed cause for schizophrenia is still unknown. Some authors such as Karon and Vandenbos (1981) claim that Freudian treatment of working through early trauma manages such cases well, though Greist et al. (1982) reflect the general psychiatric opinion that all psychotherapies today fail with psychosis.

Moreover, the causes of the other psychiatric syndromes, namely the manic affective disorders, the psychopathic or antisocial disorders, certain epilepsies and many organic brain deteriorations also remain unknown.

Not only do the supposed causes of the diseases remain unknown, but their treatments are often vague and inconclusive, even though DSM III has reduced these 'shotgun' diagnoses and treatments within the last ten years. Still, the schools of psychiatry do not yet agree on the definition of the diseases. An Englishman, for example, who is diagnosed schizophrenic in London may be termed 'over excited' or 'manic' in Los Angeles and vice versa. Fuller Torrey, who was at one time reserved about the direction of psychiatry (1974), today fully supports the biomedical approach (1983). Yet the vagueness of DSM III is apparent in his work.

Unfortunately, many patients have symptoms which place them somewhere on a spectrum between schizophrenia and manic-depressive illness. Most psychiatrists have seen individual patients who fit only one of these disease entities perfectly, but most have also seen patients with a confusing melange of symptoms of both diseases. Textbooks of psychiatry are written as if patients had one disease or the other and imply that all patients can be placed under one of the two disease categories. It has been facetiously suggested that we need either to insist that patients read the books and choose which disease they wish to have or we need to become more flexible in our psychiatric thinking. I personally have seen patients with virtually every possible combination of schizophrenic and manic-depressive symptoms (1985, 53).

To resolve some of the overlap between categories, 'schizo-affective disorders' have been defined. Treatment is somewhere in between that for schizophrenia and manic-depressive illness. This category demonstrates the lack of congruency in psychiatric treatment and its dependency upon the personality of the psychiatrist in the choice of drugs. According to Torrey,

Those who are carefully diagnosed as schizoaffective are more likely to have a good outcome to their illness, especially if they are properly treated. And proper treatment means a trial of lithium, the drug which has been used so successfully to treat manic-depressive illness. Any person with a schizoaffective disorder who has not responded to other treatment deserves a trial of lithium, and relatives of such a patient should continue shopping for a psychiatrist until they find one who uses lithium in such cases. (1983:5)

CRISIS IN TREATMENT CENTERS

Unlike a scientific revolution in the natural sciences which affects primarily an isolated group of scientists, a crisis in psychiatry is not only felt among psychiatrists but among all those confronted with the mentally ill. A common characteristic of mental health professionals in the social services and mental hospitals is demoralization and the cynical acceptance of the unsatisfactory methods of treatment for the patients. Patients are either given maintenance measures or are subjected to verbal psychotherapies, even though many of them do not respond well to talk. There is also a large measure of good-natured mothering and caring. The heroin addict is weaned on methadone, a substitute for heroin which is itself addictive. The depressed person is encouraged to talk about feelings. The manic is frequently ushered off for a 'vacation' on downers. The psychiatrist faced with a patient claiming to be the Virgin Mary, broadcasting the wisdom of God in a downtown shopping center, is likely to first search for the right drugs to quiet the patient and appease the environment. The social worker endeavors to work with the client, his impossible family conditions, his neighbors, the police and even the court system. Many of these workers feel overburdened and impotent in the face of extreme states.

In spite of increasing sophistication in research and the interconnection between chemistry and psychotic behavior, there is still no one-to-one cause and effect relationship between disease agents and cures. The applicability of disease definitions based, to a great extent, upon the experiences of a given society seems to be a dangerous definition of a 'physical' disease. A mentally healthy person in our culture is, according to medical definitions, capable of verbally relating thoughts and feelings in the absence of physical disease. Definitions in terms of given cultural norms are bound to have limited application since they are value judgements related to the observer's psychology rather than empirical reports of the client's individual language and body gestures. A qualitative classification can hardly be expected to produce quantitative changes; therefore, it is logically inconsistent to even search for quantitative causes for 'disease' which have no quantitative measures!

We have to remember that a psychotic individual has, during a psychotic episode, different values from the normal person functioning well in a society. Many severely disturbed people do not feel they are disturbed; they do not come to an analyst of their own accord. They will frequently insist that the city itself is ill. They are forced to go and seek help from the city they live in because they can no longer adapt to the financial or existential requirements of their world. Most have no interest in 'growing,' 'insight' or 'development;' they tolerate visits to a mental health professional in order to get probation, social security, financial or medical support.

Hence, we should be aware of the fact that one reason we may not be able to work well with this 'non-grower's-club' segment of the population is because our assumptions about sickness and health, insight and consciousness may not apply to them. However, it is not the logical inconsistencies in the psychiatric paradigm which inhibit its usefulness, but its inability to fulfill its goals of getting the patient healthy again and behaving like others who do not burden the city. I think it is generally accepted today that cures for the main diseases have not been found. Research based upon the description of symptoms, symptom clusters or syndromes has focused on genetic inheritence, endorphine over or under production, dysfunctional communication systems in the family of origin, neurochemistry, ethology, cognition and learning theory without being able to explain the origins of the non-organic psychoses.

It could be argued that research has still not been able to progress sufficiently to produce the desired results. Certainly inconclusive research is no argument for dropping an organizing paradigm. The above difficulties, however, give us the impression that the mental health sciences are in the midst of a typical 'pre-science' stage of development characterized by either too many or insufficient paradigms. Thus, psychiatry is in the midst of a paradigm crisis.

Chapter 2
THE PROCESS PARADIGM
IN PSYCHIATRY

The consensus view of the human being used in contemporary psychiatry is that the patient is a poor, inferior and crippled being. Torrey, one of the most respected figures in psychiatry today, says, for example, that the best way to deal with schizophrenics is to

> treat them most naturally as people. This can be verified by watching the nursing staff in any psychiatric hospital. The staff who are most respected by both professionals and patients treat the patients with dignity, and as human beings, albeit with a brain disease. (1983, p. 160)

An explorer with a beginner's mind would see the 'patient' as someone he does not understand, someone to be discovered. The process concept adds to this view the idea that to discover someone you must pay strict attention to his behavior and to the events around him. The human being in front of us is perceived correctly only when he totally agrees with our observations. Experience shows that this agreement occurs most readily when we appreciate the content of what he says, the structure of his language, the type of body signals, relationships and synchronicities associated with him.

The process approach to the individual is to find the mode of communication in which the patient is experiencing himself at a given moment, and work in that mode or channel by methods adapted to that channel. If someone is

21

hallucinating, instant communication is achieved through visualizing with him. If someone is complaining about voices, a strong intervention would be to speak in terms of the voice. If someone complains a lot about relationships, the therapist might work on his or her own feelings relative to the patient at that moment. If someone behaves in a drugged fashion, then he feels best if you use his drug-language to communicate with him. If he does not talk and looks withdrawn, then it is important to communicate with his vegetative responses.

COUPLED EFFECTS

What we observe and experience is differentiated according to the channels we observe in. Hence, you can feel something in your body such as temperature or pressure proprioceptively. You can hear voices auditorally. You can move kinesthetically. You experience people through the channel of relationship. You contact the world through synchronicity. You remember most dreams through the medium of visualization.

The activities and signals of one channel are coupled, or connected together. Hence, you may have a stomach ache, feel your stomach to be like a rock, go to sleep and dream of a rock on the ground. The proprioceptive experience of the weight in the stomach was coupled to the dream rock. And vice versa. You can dream of a volcano and have a 'splitting' headache the next day.

However, you cannot assume that if you give someone aspirin the stomach ache will go away. It frequently gets better, but because of the coupled effect, that is, because of the dreambody or the psychosomatic situation, the dream of the stone is still present and will appear again in the stomach, or in another organ. You can temporarily relieve a symptom but cannot get rid of the gestalt or archetype behind it. If the individual needs to be heavier or more like a stone, then this experience is going to try to reach consciousness in every way possible.

THE COUPLED EFFECT WITH PSYCHOPHARMICA
Hence, if you give someone medication to change his mood from depression to elation, the depressed process may or may not disappear. If it is time for the person to change his mood and to combat these moods, then the medication will also correspond to a change in behavior. If, however, the person's dreams and process of individuation want that depression for some particular reason, then medication will not work in a causal fashion because of the somatic-psychic coupling.

If you give medication to quiet down a highly aggressive patient, the medication will work only if the patient himself needs a pause from this aggression. But if the patient needs to learn how to use this aggression more consciously, he may not even take the medication in the first place.

Thus, the concept of channels and their couplings helps us to understand why it is that medication sometimes works and sometimes does not. Working only in one channel, changing proprioception through pills, body work or jogging without considering the situation in other channels, like vision or relationship, could even be dangerous. I remember the case of one patient who had fits of negativity towards everyone. His medication helped him to get along better with others, but then, in a fit of anger, he threw himself through one of the windows of his mental hospital. That negativity needed expression and should have been worked with in relationships.

The existence of coupled effects has long been recognized in the physical sciences. We need only imagine a thermo-electric effect, for example. In physics, heat is one macro-scopic process, while the flow of electricity is another. Heat up a certain material, and instead of it getting warmer, it may emit electricity and light up a bulb. Or think of another process in which you press a material and it gets warmer! Heating up a piece of material does not necessarily mean that it is going to get warmer! By the same token, giving someone psychopharmica does not necessarily mean that his mood is going to change, especially if there are coupled processes involved.

ON 'DISEASE'

Process oriented dreambody work uses the concept of disease only as it plays a role in the personal psychology of the individual. Diseases are frequently formulated by the client as enemies to overcome. Many who experience their symptoms discover them to be purposeful expressions of the human unconscious which are searching for more expression. People are, a priori, neither ill nor well in the process paradigm. Body work indicates that the body is dreaming since amplifying body symptoms seems always to produce processes which mirror what the 'sick person' is dreaming. Thus, since one always dreams, it follows that one also has many types of body experiences. Just as some dreams are pleasant and others scary, some body experiences are pleasant and others are troublesome. Being sick is a primary description of a secondary process disturbing us.

Change, in the process paradigm, occurs through the confrontation of awareness with processes trying to unfold. Since many processes cannot unfold completely, they spin in mid-air, like a wheel not touching the ground. This spinning may be experienced as a relationship problem, a body symptom, a dream, a neurosis, a psychosis or combinations of all of these expressions.

ON TERMS

To ease communication between us, I will continue to use terms belonging to other paradigms such as 'conscious' and 'unconscious' (depth psychology), 'sickness' and 'health' (medicine), 'sanity' and 'insanity' (legal terms), 'mental disorder,' 'schizophrenia,' 'sociopathy' (psychiatry), etc. I attempt to define these words in terms of process concepts and show how they may be limiting cases of the more neutral paradigm. The reader interested in a brief explanation of the interrelationship between psychiatric and process terms may turn to the Glossary at the end of this book for reference.

The terminology I develop is based upon my interest in dealing with strongly altered and unusual states of consciousness and upon my phenomenological approach to these states. Older terms such as 'withdrawn' and 'related' are not useful in actually understanding the structure of processes, especially when these are very foreign to everyday life. Hence, psychiatry needs a new language, one which deals with events as they occur, in contrast to a language which is strongly biased to consensus reality thinking. Thus, I will have to speak of 'primary and secondary processes,' 'channels,' 'double signals' and other terms which are not common in psychology today. I hope the reader will understand and bear with me.

Let us call *primary processes* those expressions with which the individual identifies himself either explicitly or implicitly. Someone who implies or says, 'I am the Virgin Mary,' or 'I am a rock star or a business woman,' indicates that her primary process is an identity experience of the Virgin, a rock star or business person. Primary processes can be identified even in strongly altered states of consciousness.

Secondary processes refer to all other processes which an individual does not experience as belonging to him, and which he speaks about as if they happened to him from the outside, or as caused by another agent. For example, 'My leg is killing me,' 'The police are after me,' 'The world is against me,' or 'This other person helps me,' etc. are statements which express that the leg, the police, the world and a helper are the names of secondary processes. These processes are further from awareness; they are projected and experienced outside of the individual who expresses them. Both primary and secondary processes are only partially conscious.

The individual identity is connected to the primary process. *Consciousness* is a term which I use only for those moments in which the individual is aware of primary and secondary processes. Consciousness refers to a reflective awareness, to the existence of a *metacommunicator*, someone who is able to talk about his experiences and perceptions.

I use the term *double signals* to refer to expressions coming from a person which are part of his secondary processes, information with which he is not able to identify himself in a given moment. The reader interested in the background to these terms is referred to the first chapter of *River's Way*.

PRACTICAL CONSEQUENCES OF PROCESS THEORY

Change happens through or is associated with the unfolding of patterns. This means, for example, that a man who is constantly moody or a woman who tends to fall into a cool nastiness towards others will not necessarily change through insight into dream material alone. Empirical knowledge indicates that insight is most effective when it follows experience; it is then likely to coincide with change.

In the analytical paradigm, for example, the man will dream about his moodiness or the woman about her coldness and this dream material will be discussed, interpreted and related to present or past situations. In the process paradigm, the dreamer will be encouraged to become aware of aspects of himself which are close to and distant from awareness (namely primary and secondary processes), and to follow their process of unravelling.

For example, someone dreams about an explosion and has a stomach ache. If this stomach ache is experienced as something trying to break out, it is a relatively constant occurrence in process work that the stomach ache will turn out to mirror the dream, showing the individual that a part of him is trying to explode. By experiencing this more completely, either through visualizing it, hearing it, feeling it, acting it out, noticing it in relationships or synchronicities, consciousness and change happen simultaneously.

PROCESS ELEMENTS IN MODERN SCHOOLS

The Freudian encouraging her patient to experience her transference is encouraging insight through process work. The Jungian who uses active imagination to meet dream figures on paper is using a process paradigm. The Gestalt therapist requiring her client to act out a dream is dramatizing an experience which has been secondary. The neo-Reichian working through resistances to aggression in body work is touching the process work paradigm if these resistances are allowed to express themselves and are not simply 'broken through.' The process paradigm is not new; it plays a crucial role in all psychotherapies, and is accepted as a basic concept everywhere in psychology. The process paradigm may even be considered a central pattern in our earliest sciences. Alchemy is based upon cooking what is incomplete and Taoism encourages one to discover the patterns behind reality and to follow their unfolding with appreciation and awareness.

My background in process work is based upon the finalistic philosophy applied by Jung to psychological situations. He looked for the meaning of things; he was not interested in pathologizing them, but attempted to take them as facts for themselves. Since he was himself a physician he recognized the usefulness of the medicial model, but extended it by concentrating on the fantasy world produced by the client.

RESERVATIONS ABOUT PROCESS WORK

Process oriented psychology differs from more popular 'process psychologies' in its differentiated method of observation. Thus, a frequent misunderstanding derived from popular conceptions of the term 'process' is that clients can get dangerously or uselessly wrapped up in their 'process,' that is, get too involved in themselves. Would it not be more useful and valuable at times to simply give direct and clear instructions which a client could follow?

Encouraging clients to follow only one part of themselves is always less useful then helping them contact all their parts. Only the total process is really healing. Following a client in process oriented psychology means not only following the part which the client identifies with in the moment, but following the total process, that is, with both primary and secondary signals.

Thus, encouraging a client to be God when he is proclaiming that he is God and that the 'authorities' are evil would be less useful than enabling him to get in contact with his own inner authorities. Once this is done, he will be able to take simple and helpful directions from others and will even be able to give them to himself. As long as he is identified with God, it is not likely he will be able to hear or follow such instructions.

Until recently, contacting the other side of a polarization during an acute episode has been difficult to achieve with patience and psychological interventions alone, that is, without drugs. The following chapters present psychological interventions which may contribute to reducing the need for such drugs.

INTRODUCTION TO THE SOCIAL WORK PROJECT
In this work I am going to investigate the usefulness of the process oriented paradigm in relationship to 'difficult' clients. Clients come more or less spontaneously to the social service station where this project took place. Instead of going to their normal social worker, psychologist, or financial advisor, the clients seeking help from the station were invited to sit together with me and my colleague, Dr Joe Goodbread, the whole social work team, including secretaries, social workers and bosses, and also with my video camera which was taping the entire transaction.

The video taping was explained to all involved as an attempt to improve my understanding of the client's behavior and to help the team in their work. I asked the clients to help us with this. Their response was almost unanimously positive. They enjoyed the team atmosphere to such an extent that most wanted to come back again soon. The break in the normal one-to-one relationship with their therapists was met at first with apprehension, but soon the jovial and loose atmosphere relaxed everyone. Each client felt appreciated and important sitting with the group of therapists and social workers.

During the hour-long sessions there were between three and eleven people present. Some meetings included every-one interested in a given client, city officials, the head of the regional social work services, social workers who had just dropped in to see what was happening and who wanted to learn more, and of course the Dubendorf team itself. The focus of communication was placed, for the most part, upon the client. The different therapists were encouraged to bring in their separate reactions. I found all of these reactions meaningful and even felt at times as if each of those present was necessary.

These therapists had never worked together in such a way before. I found that they relieved one another, complemented one another, augmented and in some cases mirrored the patient's process. There would always be one therapist interested in getting the client a job, helping him into this reality, and another who would try to mother him and communicate with feeling. Still another wanted to get to the root of what was happening. All were necessary. The problems which arose, were, I believe, typical of clients and social work agencies everywhere.

Their leader's report after the supervision week stated, 'We presented our supervisor with our fourteen most difficult cases and discovered that if there were any limits to his approach, they did not appear in the present cases.' Once the original excitement of the seminar had passed, this enthusiastic report was tempered by the everyday reality of the client, his long history of problems, and the difficulties involved in employing the process oriented paradigm without thorough training in signal work.

The problems involved in working with severely disturbed people were a combination of what the team experienced as 'tricks and traps' of the clients, pressure from the client's environment to make him more adapted, internal stress between the team members, internal difficulties of each individual on the team, and a lack of training in signal awareness. A quasi-medical approach to the patient of viewing him as if he had a brain disease often clouded accurate perceptions. Furthermore, difficulties arose which were outside the scope of the video taping, difficulties involving interactions with the client's neighbors, police and court. In addition, I realize now in retrospect, after having spent hundreds of hours studying and transcribing the case material, that I, too, learned a lot about where I needed to learn more. There were times I wasted energy conflicting with instead of following the client. Frequently things happened so quickly that I was not able to understand the process structure until after having studied the tapes.

METHODS

The basic process paradigm is that signals and information from the client-therapist pair contain their own structure and implicit evolution, that is, the solutions to the problems at hand. The method was to wait to develop a strategy until the structure had become apparent.

When working with people with whom I have trouble communicating, I always refer to my video tape recording. I often make decisions only after having studied the video in order to discover which information I have not allowed myself to pick up and why I did not pick it up. If the client becomes increasingly unhappy during the session or afterwards, or if my communication to the client does not receive a favorable response, I assume that I have to change. I usually find out that I have rigid conceptions of how people should be or am unconscious of something I am projecting onto the client which makes it impossible for me either to pick up or to deal openly with what is happening. For example, in one sitting where a woman suffering from chronic alcoholism spoke about what seemed to me to be a harmful interaction with her little children, I entered a cyclical and antagonist process with her in which I was anything but helpful, either to her or those around her. She brought up problems in myself I first had to deal with before I was even able to understand the video tape.

This particular woman helped me to be definitive about my own goals in working with her and others, and helped me to become aware of the occasional discrepancy between what the therapist's and client's goals may be. As far as I know, my goals seem to be (i) to achieve what I interpret to be unequivocal positive response from the client, (2) to get the same response from the environment, (3) to enjoy myself to the utmost, and (4) to appreciate the nature of difficult situations. Obviously I have to be wide awake about myself because not every client will automatically join me in these expectations!

Part II
SCHIZOPHRENIA

Chapter 3
THE MISSING
METACOMMUNICATOR

The definition of schizophrenia depends upon the school of psychiatry and the treatment. Thus if physical factors such as inheritance are considered (Freedman et al., 1980, p. 421), then the bio-model is used. When relationships are focused upon, the psychodynamic-interaction model arises. Such a model can be seen in Freud's (1950) description of schizophrenia as a 'deep, primary disturbance of a patient's object relationships, a narcissistic psychosis which precludes psychotherapy' because the patient is not ready for transference relations. The phenomenological-existential model understands the patient strictly within the limits of his own self-evidence. There are conditioning-behavior models which demonstrate that the disease is connected to acquired responses and sociological models indicating that schizophrenia is produced by urban ghettos. A 'vulnerability stress' theory combines English, American and Swiss-German research as well as biomedical considerations and social dynamics (Schweizerische Aerzte Zeitung, Band 66, Heft 34, August 1985).

Though there is no one generally accepted definition of schizophrenia, Bleuler's (1950) original definition seems to prevail in European psychiatry text books. Bleuler diagnosed schizophrenia from symptoms characterized by disturbances of thinking, affect and volition. Schizophrenia means, literally, a splitting of the mind. Bleuler observed that the initiative of the patient is split into several potentialities. Thoughts and associations are fragmented and 'devoid of meaning,' indicating a lack of apparent logic. Affect is no longer 'adequate or appropriate' to a given situation. Though there is no loss of memory, no obvious physical cause and adequate time and space orientation, Bleuler pointed out that the schizophrenic has difficulty distinguishing between internal and external reality. There is frequently an early and gradual onset between the ages of fifteen to thirty.

According to DSM III, schizophrenia is diagnosed only when the following criteria are fulfilled:

1 Symptoms of illness have been present for at least six months.
2 There has been some deterioration of functioning from previous levels in such areas as work skills, social relations and self-care.
3 The disease began before age 45.
4 The disease symptoms do not suggest organic mental disorders or mental retardation.
5 The disease symptoms do not suggest the manic-depressive illness (bi-polar illness).
6 At least one of the following symptoms is present:
  a Bizarre delusions where the content is patently absurd and has no possible basis in fact, such as delusions of being controlled, thought insertion, thought withdrawal and thought broadcasting.
  b Delusions of a grandiose, religious, nihilistic or somatic nature if ideas of persecution are absent.
  c Delusions of persecution or jealous content if accompanied by hallucinations of any type.
  d Auditory hallucinations in which a voice comments on a person's behavior or thoughts, or two or more voices converse with each other.
  e Auditory hallucinations heard on several occasions with content of more than one or two words and having no apparent relation to depression or elation.
  f Marked loosening of associations, markedly illogicial thinking, incoherence or marked poverty of speech if associated with either blunted or inappropriate

affect, delusions, hallucinations, catatonia or grossly disorganized behavior.

Diagnosis is obviously still a subjective factor which depends upon the personality and values of the observer. It is often difficult to determine what thought withdrawal or inappropriate feeling is since many people have 'unusual' feeling relationships. Schizophrenia is usually meant to mean the coexistence of disparate affects and behavior, for example, giggling and then killing someone, having a pleasant evening, giving everyone a warm goodbye and then committing suicide, yelling happily and stripping in church, etc.

AN EXAMPLE OF PROCESS WORK

Instead of discussing schizophrenia in general terms, let me introduce Herr E., a man who has been diagnosed with schizophrenia and has been in and out of mental hospitals for many years. Every Monday morning he appears punctually at 8.00 am as the doors to the social service station open in order to collect his weekly disability payment.

As he walks in, I am informed that he has been hospitalized many times and is once again being considered for hospitalization because he has been disturbing the city authorities with incoherent complaints. In his folder I see he has been writing many letters to the police accusing the social work agencies of having cheated him out of money. There are over forty letters in the file. The letters, however, are unconvincing because the logic is difficult to follow. As he enters the room, I notice that Herr E. is over six feet tall, heavily set, moves slowly and powerfully and speaks with a deep voice, expressing himself vehemently and what seems to me a bit menacing. The following is a verbatim transcription and translation from Swiss-German of the interview with Herr E., the staff director, Dan and myself.

Herr E.: I am looking for work in town, in private industry, with a temporary office.

Arny: What sort of work do you do?
Herr E.: It depends upon what they produce.
Arny: I understand.

I nod encouragingly so that he will go on speaking though I do not know to what 'they' refers.

Herr E.: I have no patience. They give me no money for vacation. Nevertheless I make vacation at home.
Arny: Yes.
Herr E.: Doing, understanding . . . I have written the criminal police often for help and for money. This social work boss sitting here [nodding towards Dan] is not healthy. He reads . . . in the newspapers. The newspaper is no longer coming to me. He and the insurance people steal money from me. I have no time to work. I am busy. . . .

As Herr E. speaks, he sits forward aggressively moving his hands in front of Dan and me and then sits back, acting as if he is listening. Then he sits forward and speaks angrily again, saying to me,

Herr E.: They are dishonest, they are not healthy, they need help, check them out, don't just inspect them, help them.

The movements forwards and backwards in his chair occur at intervals of approximately sixty seconds. A typical statement when he sits back is

Herr E.: I have no time to work. I don't like it exactly. Now I am on vacation.

PROCESS STRUCTURE
It is difficult to understand Herr E. in terms of conscious and unconscious, for everything he does seems to be unconscious. If, however, we resist using these terms, we can ask questions with more quantitative answers. What process

does he identify himself with? What process does he experience as being outside of himself or as happening to him?

He identifies himself as being on vacation. He doesn't like working and has no time for it. He is angry at the authorities for not giving him money for vacation. This 'vacationer,' let us say, is his primary process, the one he identifies with.

His secondary process, the process with which he is in conflict and which he experiences as happening to him from the outside, is the 'unhealthy' social worker. The authorities are sick, steal from him and need help. The vacationer is well but the authorities, in his opinion, are sick. It is important that Herr E. sees only the 'others' as ill; he, as the vacationer, is in order. We will return to this statement later on.

OBJECTLESS PROJECTIONS
We should be careful in thinking that the actual authorities are as dreadful as he imagines. Naturally, many people do not like city authorities because some of them really are difficult to deal with and sometimes even disturbed. Herr E.'s authorities, however, are not identified with a specific group or individual. These authorities are a 'field,' an idea, a piece of his psyche, so to speak, hanging in mid-air waiting to find an object. Anyone who criticizes or resists him can and will fill the authority role.

For example, he said that Dan, the director of the social service station, is not well. But two minutes later, when I get tough with him and accuse him of being lazy, I become the critical, resistant authority and Dan is relieved of this projection. Herr E. defends himself against me when I challenge his statement about not wanting to work.

Arny: I think you may be lazy.
Herr E.: This man here, this Dan, he is a very good guardian. He will take care of me until I get to be 65. The law says he is really good. He must see that I live to 65.

ON 'INAPPROPRIATE FEELING'

We see from this short section of the work that Herr E. does not relate to me or to Dan with any degree of continuity. One- moment we are good, the next we are bad. Our positions change in his mind since his momentary behavior is independent of what has been felt or said a moment before. At one moment Dan is unhealthy and then in the next he is wonderful. Because the past is unimportant for him in his communication, we feel that he does not relate to us. What we are perceiving is that he relates more to an inner system than to our need for logical understanding. Hence, it is tempting to call him 'unrelated' or say that his affect is 'disturbed.' These judgements imply that 'inappropriate' and 'unrelated' are absolute characteristics instead of relative ones connected to our models of communication.

FEEDBACK AND LOOPS

A more quantitative way of speaking about his behavior is to notice that he does not adjust his opinions about us according to what we do. Dan has not changed towards him. Yet Herr E.'s feeling has changed towards Dan. Herr E. has only a minimal feedback loop; either he does not pick up or does not adjust to outer signals.

The short section which I have presented from our interview is typical for many diagnosed schizophrenics. A process oriented description would not call them sick but would describe their particular process as having a special kind of signal feedback loop in relationship to others. The meaning and significance of this loop remains to be investigated.

THE MEANING OF NOT PICKING UP FEEDBACK

One characteristic of a missing feedback loop is that it gives the individual process the appearance of being a field with two states. The two states in Herr E.'s field are the vacationer and the unhealthy authority. The unusual characteristic of this process in contrast to the majority of other processes is that this field is unpopulated by real, living people. In other words, the authority figures are not projected onto specific people but are object-less projections. At one moment Dan is a sick authority and in the next he is a well-meaning guardian and I become the nasty authority. Herr E. does not notice that Dan has not changed towards him. Thus Herr E. has a process without a feedback loop and appears to be a psyche with two states floating in mid-air, a field looking for people, so to speak.

What appears as inappropriate feeling, then, could be seen as an attempt to relate only to an inner process, one in which a story is trying to unfold about a city dweller fighting the authorities. A psychoanalytical interpretation would say that Herr E. is using a projection mechanism (a projective identification) to split off a part of his past and work it out in the present through Dan. From an analytical perspective, Herr E. is working on a collective archetype, akin to the story of the hero overthrowing the old and ailing king.

The lack of feedback, however, is not a pathological feature, but one which can also be seen in non-psychotics as well. Having no feedback loop makes Herr E. unconscious of certain objective, environmental phenomena by filtering out signals which oppose his belief in order to preserve and complete the inner story or myth he is working on. In other words, having no feedback loop functions to keep him in his own dream world, and this is a function of unconsciousness which can be observed in all of us. Such loops are at work all the time, even in the therapist, as I will soon show.

THE THERAPIST AND PATIENT IN THE SAME BOAT

The therapist or theoretical paradigm which claims that the patient has inappropriate feeling because he does not react in an 'appropriate' manner suffers from unconsciousness in exactly the same way as the patient. I have seen many professionals telling their clients that they have brain disease or that their problems are due to a particular illness while the patient looks down at the floor or out of the window. If the therapist would react 'appropriately,' i.e. with feedback to these signals, she would realize that her diagnosis of the patient gets little or no feedback from the patient. If the therapist does not react to this feedback and adjust her therapeutic behavior to the patient's negative signals, then she, too, lacks a feedback loop.

What is the function of the therapist's unconsciousness? It has helped her to formulate medical theories and to discover chemical origins and connections to mental diseases. Hence, it has helped to keep us in a medical myth in order to reach completion. But this unconsciousness should be coming to an end. We should note that telling a patient he is ill is not an appropriate belief if the patient does not agree. At the very least we should see that we, too, have no feedback loop to large parts of reality.

METACOMMUNICATION

Lacking a feedback loop is not sufficient criterion for an extreme or psychotic state. To understand the difference between Herr E.'s process and the ones we normally meet, we need one more concept: metacommunication.

This fancy term means communicating about some aspect of communication. Metacommunication is the ability to comment on a message, its sender or its effect. For example, if I am able to metacommunicate. I can communicate about my communication signals, what I say, how I say it, whether or not I feel the receiver has understood, the reason I have spoken, etc. Herr E. cannot metacommunicate; he cannot talk about the way he is communicating, or what it is he is saying. Thus he cannot comment on his communicative mode to say that he is projecting or dreaming.

METACOMMUNICATION AND THE GROWER'S CLUB

One of the basic paradigms of classical analysis is that there is always someone present in the patient to metacommunicate. This means that the therapist assumes that the client is interested in or will eventually be interested in dreams, relationships, body experiences and therapeutic strategies.

Most of the time, patients coming to psychotherapy are capable of and interested in metacommunicating. These people and their therapists belong to what I call the 'grower's club:' those interested in growth, development and insight. Like most club members everywhere members of the grower's club are prejudiced against non-members. Great numbers of our population, however, do not belong to the grower's club, and furthermore, they need not belong. They have other processes. Some of those people called schizophrenics and many other psychotic individuals do not belong to this club. They do not like to, are not able to, or think it is ridiculous to talk about their communication and their states. Moreover most of you reading this paragraph right now are capable of metacommunicating only some of the time. I myself, for example, hate to metacommunicate about anger while I am in the midst of it. I try, but do not always succeed.

THE AVAILABLE METACOMMUNICATOR:
NORMAL AND PSYCHOTIC

Thus, the terms 'normal' and 'psychotic' can be more accurately defined by terms which enable one to work with the processes at hand. The 'normal' person metacommunicates. Temporarily, in an extreme state, he does not. *The 'psychotic person' does not metacommunicate for long periods of time.* There is no third party available to talk about either his primary or secondary process. No one is 'at home' to comment on intelligent interpretations. There is no one there, for the moment at least, who is interested in or cares to discuss a given therapeutic strategy. By 'no one,' I mean that there is no one available. After coming out of extreme states, many people will say that they felt 'the observer' was underwater or in a back room. Since there is a wide continuum of time spans in which an available metacommunicator is absent, reaching from a given moment to long periods of time, we see that psychosis refers, in most cases, to a temporary state capable of change.

THE AWARENESS PRINCIPLE

The question of the usefulness of having no metacommunicator remains. The hologram, anthropos and field theories of the world, the concepts of the evolving universe in physics and of the hologram-like brain in biology

(Pribram: 1981, indicate a world operating like a field or unit (see *The Dreambody in Relationships*, Chapter 7). Anthropos theories give us the idea that this field has an awareness of its own.

A useful and tentative theory to consider is that a field does everything it can to bring itself to consciousness. People normally experience this in their personal lives when they become aware of experiences which make life more meaningful. In the case of an extreme psychotic state, however, there is no one at home to pick up the information, no one except the environment, that is. A useful hypothesis is that the field in which we live uses people like Herr E., people with no metacommunicator, to express itself to the rest of the world. His inability to work with his process forces us to confront it. We are pressed to formulate theories and think about issues we would otherwise neglect.

The field thus informs the general public about its conflicts. This can be formulated in different ways, depending upon belief systems. One might say that the Self wants to know itself, or that God is trying to discover himself, the Anthropos we are living in is trying to wake up, the collective unconscious is trying to express itself or the universe is evolving in such a way as to make us more aware of the meaning of life.

In the present case, the field problem being expressed is a collective conflict of Switzerland. It is the problem between the vacationer or tourist and the hard-working Swiss governed by the motto that 'Work and Prayer Make Life Sweet.' In Switzerland, relaxing is a main source of income but also a great problem for a country where bureaucracy and discipline rate high on the national scale of good and bad.

GOALS, TREATMENT AND PROCESS WORK
One goal in dealing with Herr E. is to change him so that he stops being a lazy vacationer, learns how to metacommunicate about his problems and leaves the social service agencies in peace. Though this goal will be shared by the

social work authorities, the police and most Swiss, it is a one-sided goal because it does not match Herr E.'s own goals.

Process work's immediate aim is to understand and unravel the processes at hand. This matches closely what Herr E. wants. He feels he needs more peace and quiet and more money to do this with. But he cannot achieve his goals beause of the inner and outer authorities who are unhealthy and need help.

In what follows, we will work with Herr E.'s inner authorities and show how to improve their 'health,' while simultaneously recommending a method of working with the outer ones as well.

Chapter 4
WORKING WITH A
SCHIZOPHRENIC STATE

In the last chapter we talked about the psychology of
Herr E. Here I want to concentrate on developing techniques for working with him in an extreme state.

To work with Herr E. we need more information about his
process structure and behavior. I have already mentioned
that the two processes, the vacationer and the authority, are
in conflict with one another. His lack of a readily available
metacommunicator has also been discussed.

FLIP-FLOPPING
On the video tape of the interview with Herr E., the
authority can be seen in his continual moving forward and
the vacationer is present when he sits backward. This dual
process occurs about every sixty seconds. The authority sits
forward, calculates aggressively with a red face and tries,
usually with insufficient logic, to make his point.

This flip-flopping is characteristic of processes in which
there is no available metacommunicator to hold, consider or
present any one of the parts. When two parts either follow
each other in rapid sequence or are simultaneously superimposed upon one another, it is due to the lack of such an
observer.

For example, when Herr E. says, 'I haven't time to work. I
am on vacation and must get up at 5.00 in order to do my
wash,' we hear two, almost simultaneous contradictory
statements without the experience of paradox from the
communicator. 'I have no time to work,' and then, 'I have to

get up at 5.00 to do my wash,' means, I suspect, that he has no time to work because he is working so much at something else, presumably his inner material. With some consideration, we can almost always make logical meaning out of his statement, but at first inspection it appears that he has no time to work because he is working too much.

NO DOUBLE SIGNALS

When he says this conflicting statement, he does not appear to be in conflict with himself. He is simply angry at the authorities for not letting him go on vacation. From someone else, we would expect a more conventional reaction to such a statement, namely one in which he giggles or blushes, embarrassed about wanting to get up at 5.00 am to wash. The giggle would represent the availability of another part which realizes the absurdity of what he is saying. A person with a metacommunicator would feel guilty for only wanting to 'do his wash.' But Herr E. does not giggle; he does not double signal at all. Instead he has a terrifying congruence, a convincing quality and single-pointedness about what he is doing and saying since he does not ostensibly suffer from the paradoxical nature of his statements. The reason he does not suffer is because suffering entails the presence of a metacommunicator, someone aware of conflicts. Such a communicator or sufferer is not available with Herr E.

TERRIFYING CONGRUITY

Since there is no metacommunicator, there is no conflict between processes and they superimpose or flip-flop from one to another without reserve. This can have disastrous consequences for the environment. A person in such an extreme and unusual state may be smiling at you, suddenly hear a voice which says he should chop off a child's head and then, without reflecting or inhibiting himself, actually kill a child.

Such incidents do not happen often, but they are frequent enough to be mentioned. The therapist should not think, however, that these incidents are unpredictable; the voice was actually signalled months before. His voices had told him to murder the child more than once. The therapist working with this client had not sufficiently respected the secondary murder process. In at least one way people who go through psychotic episodes could be less dangerous than 'normal' people since normal people hide their secondary processes more successfully!

AN EARLY EXPERIENCE

Since my first contact with a diagnosed schizophrenic some twenty-five years ago, I have learned to treat secondary processes with great respect. My first schizophrenic patient was a man in a wild and ecstatic condition (he could have been manic), radiating in all his glory and grinning at me. I was terrified. He said, 'I am Lucifer, the bringer and destroyer of light.' I was just beginning my practice at the time and thought, 'He is just crazy.' I do not remember if I told him what I thought, but he looked me straight in the eye and said, 'And since you do not believe me, watch what I can do now.' At that moment the lights in my house went out. The fuses had not blown. Call it chance, synchronicity or anything you like, but it cured my inflation of thinking that I was real and sane and he was just crazy. Every signal is real! The best working hypothesis is to believe in and try to understand people's signals.

PROCESS WORK WITH HERR E.

To work with Herr E., I took the following information which he gave me into consideration. He had said, 'Do not talk to the authority, work with him, help him, he is sick.' I saw the flip-flop nature of his process and its instability. I imagined that previous to his psychosis, his identity was probably close to what he now called the authorities. I wanted to work with this 'authority,' to get to this part which was so heavily projected onto the world around him. Accessing this part would enable me to unravel its existence in order to help it.

OCCUPATION THEORY

The experience with normal individual processes indicates that if two people are present in a field in which there is an authority figure and a vacationer (a bad and good figure or any other polarity), then one person will become an authority figure, like I did at one point, while the second person – even though he had previously been the authority – will become the good guy or the vacationer. The occupation theory states that the one who is momentarily most authoritarian becomes the authority, while the weaker one becomes the vacationer. This is true for any polarized system. (See *The Dreambody in Relationships*.)

This is also the rule with families and groups. The part any given individual plays in a system is determined by what other parts are occupied. In other words, if there is no authority in a group which has a pattern of the weaker one versus the authority, then either one of the weaker people will automatically begin acting authoritarian or else the authority will be projected onto a person not present.

Since Herr E.'s pattern is the vacationer *v.* the authority, the way to get the authority to appear is, theoretically, to play the vacationer even better than Herr E. does. This should bring out the authority. This is exactly what I did with my colleague Joe's help. I took home the video tape and studied the vacationer in great detail. The next time Herr E. came to the social work center, next Monday at 8.00 am, I greeted him using the facial expression of the vacationer, his hand motion (putting them into my pockets the way he did), his sentences and tone, in short, imitating the vacationer as much as possible.

Arny: Hi, how are you? I am on vacation, and have no time to work. I am too busy for that and want my money, and damn it, have to wait here until I get it.

Herr E.:   Well, if you want to get a job, then you must first go to the office which has jobs, then you must. . . .

He seemed to forget that I was there to supervise the social work agency (no feedback loop!). He became an authority for me and gave me, in the most convincing and congruent fashion, information about Swiss laws and how to get a job. He even told me about work permits in the country. When I complained about my lack of money, he reached deeply into his own pocket and brought out some change which he gave me to call the social work office responsible for helping people obtain jobs. Several days after this interaction I received the following letter from him:

Dear Arnold Mindell,
Please realize that Switzerland has a 44 hour week and that you should contact the Labor Department at ____ for work, naturally after first trying to get a job for yourself. Please consider the last firm I worked for, they are reliable.

Sincerely yours,
Herr E.

On the back of this letter was a copy of his last job contract. His letter was legible – more than my writing is – though not particularly neat.

MORAL CONSIDERATIONS

Before delving into Herr E.'s advice, I want to consider the philosophical implications of psychological interventions. By accessing the authority figure, I have been successful only in a collective light. I have got Herr E. to behave normally, that is, like the rest of us. This is possible to do with everyone in his condition for shorter or longer periods of time. The advantage in having done this is that now the original primary process of Herr E. can be worked with and this part can decide what should be happening in the future.

This part is the part which agrees with the rest of the world that the schizophrenic is a sick person. It should be noted that only 13 per cent of the schizophrenics in a given study (Torrey, 1983, p. 185) felt that they were ill – I assume as long as they were in their vacationer or anti-social process. Hence, we have not done anyone a real favor by accessing the 'normal' or social part of the personality, and it is dangerous to think that we have been successful because such thinking neglects the patient's primary process, Herr E.'s vacationer, who thinks that he is well and the authorities are sick!

The advantage of having accessed the normal part is that now both parts are more available to the patient and both can be worked with. Now he may be able to make a decision about his own future. After three or four days of intensive work, every schizophrenic patient I have seen came out of their extreme state. At this point many patients decide that they hated their episode and want only to go back to normal life. They remain in their normal life ever after. Others will come back with another episode after as long as ten years. Still others will stay with psychotherapy at this point and begin to integrate their vacationer or other extreme states while holding on to their social personality.

But each to his own. Some patients return to their extreme state after only days, saying as one woman said to me, 'Doctor, it was so beautiful to be on the moon. I was so happy there, why do you torture me by asking me to live in your harsh world? I do not have the strength to bear it here.' Several hours later she was back in the psychosis once again with a euphoric expression lecturing to all about the moon and other planets. Who is to say that she should be in a different place? She had a choice, made a decision, and kept to it.

I have heard of other cases in which the physician gave a patient drugs, brought him out of his extreme episode only to report the resulting suicide.

An elderly gentleman I treated had been living alone with only his 'devils' (auditory hallucinations) for companionship for many years. After carefully adjusting his medication we were able to get rid of the 'devils,' at which point he fully realized how lonely and isolated he was and he drowned himself. Given the symptom-caused torment

and social isolation which many schizophrenics must
endure, in truth I find it surprising that the suicide rate
among them is not higher than it is. (Torrey, 1983, p. 174)

What this doctor does not mention is the possibility that the
schizophrenic had his 'devils' as friends; his extreme state
gave life meaning and prevented him from dying. Without
the devils, it is fully possible that there was no longer any
reason to live. Or, it is possible that one of his devils was no
longer friendly to him and helped him to drown! Or, it
could also be possible that the medication blocked the
auditory channel through altering neurotransmitters so that
the devils were no longer located there but took over his
movement, whereupon he killed himself. I do not know
what happened, but I would like the reader to suffer some
of the philosophical uncertainties involved in working with
psychotic states. My philosophy is doubt and observe, try to
follow the individual process as closely as possible.

EVALUATION
Now let us go back to the details of Herr E.'s situation.
Playing the vacationer constellated the authority in him
relative to me because he did not have the feedback loop to
adjust his behavior to changes in mine. This produced the
authority and showed the areas in the authority figure
(Herr E.'s letter was incomplete) which needed working on.

His writing was not particularly neat, for example. This
would need to be worked on. While maintaining the role of
vacationer, I would simultaneously be the therapist and get
the authority to be neater and more exact about his times
and dates by asking the authority to adjust himself and his
information to my particular sort of 'work problems.' This is
what continued therapy along these lines would look like.

This plan would have to be adjusted to changes which
occur. As he changes, I would have to change. The same
process structure, namely the vacationer and the authority, is
likely to change after the flip is completed, then other
processes will come up resembling the processes normally
dealt with in psychotherapy. I have focused mainly upon

the extreme state, since this is the one felt to be inaccessible to classical psychotherapeutic intervention. Process reversals usually relieve the patient and simultaneously allow the healing paradigm of medicine to function without tampering with the patient's neurochemistry.

AN EXAMPLE

I remember a client I worked with who first came to me calling herself the Virgin Mary. Apparently she had had many such episodes before. She came from simple European peasant surroundings. In the midst of the extreme state, her secondary process was the 'evil mother' of the world who hated Christianity and had no interest in her. 'The evil mother cannot support the Christ Child, my child,' she said. Moreover, she identified the doctors and clinics as being evil mothers. I still recall how she flipped back into her old process. When I played the Virgin Mary, she became a typical negative mother, uninterested in the fantasies of her child. She said to me, forgetting I was the therapist, 'Be careful dear, if you continue in that mad euphoria, you will either end up in the nut house or I will put you there.'

She regained and subsequently retained the 'evil mother of the world' personality which she previously had, to the contentment of those around her – her physician, husband and neighbors. What had been her secondary process during the episode now became her primary one; she was an evil mother towards her own fantasies and her episode and detested herself for having gone through such states. For the time being then, the Virgin Mary who loves all became her secondary process with no possibility of being integrated into the primary one. The result was that she simply turned cold to those around her and left it up to the rest of us to integrate the Virgin Mary who supports divine religious experience. She liked being back in her normal state. I realized that the work was incomplete, because the Virgin had not been integrated into her daily life. Several years later she came back with a very mild version of the first episode, this time prepared to put her parts together.

LIMITATIONS

Process work's limitation is that it requires a thorough knowledge of signals and the ability to differentiate between them in order to discover the process structure organizing behavior. Learning this takes several years.

Moreover, dramatizing the primary process of the person in a flipped state is not every therapist's cup of tea. It requires not only signal study but also the ability to feel into and act out these signals. One need not be a perfect actor because the individual in an extreme state reacts (according to occupation theory) to the mere attempt to act out the primary process. This attempt is almost always sufficient to bring out the necessary change.

TRAINING

Complete understanding of a client requires observation and action coming from the heart. But this will not be enough for an individual in an extreme state or acute psychotic episode because people in these states filter out signals which do not directly fit into the drama of their inner life. This lack of reactivity to normal communication is one of the reasons which have made mind-altering drugs the choice of many therapists.

To get into the world of the psychotic episode without drugs, the therapist will have to learn how to clearly see, feel and act out the primary process of the client. This gives her the chance to get out of the polarization which makes the rest of the world the denied part of the personality, the secondary process. Without the ability to act out the primary process, the therapist's understanding of what the client is going through is bound to be judgemental, intellectual or inhibited by diagnostic thinking. Value judgements cannot be hidden and are always felt by the client who reacts frequently by discontinuing potential long-term therapy.

I recommend to all those interested in trying to understand psychotic states to experiment with their own extreme situations. Each of us has two parts, one we identify with and one which is in our dreams and body experiences. The schizophrenic episode is known to all. Just act out the secondary process and make a discovery: it is a great relief to 'flip' sides! Then ask a friend to act out your flipped side better than you are doing and you will experience flipping back to 'normal.'

THE THERAPIST'S TOLERANCE

Most people in extreme states will claim that the part which seems normal to the therapist – in Herr E.'s case, the authority figure – is sick. This is the exact opposite of what the normal therapist thinks, namely that the patient's primary process – in the present case, the vacationer – is the disturbed one. Hence process work is difficult because it requires a relatively objective and simultaneously emotional involvement in the client's process. If you try to change the vacationer (or convince a client that he or she is not the Virgin Mary, etc.) or if you try to change what is defined as being well, you are going to run into unnecessary resistances and will probably fail to achieve either your own or your client's goals.

ON RAPPORT WITH PARTS

Another difficulty with process work is that the therapist has to be aware of her own reactions to the parts of her client. Negative reactions to parts like the vacationer or the Virgin Mary are usually 'dreamed up,' that is, they are opinions which belong to the client's own secondary process, or previous identity – in our case the authority or evil mother. If you unconsciously become a part of someone's process, you have no viewpoint outside the field and consequently lose your objective ability to work with it. The typical psychiatrist who feels that the patient's fantasies are ridiculous and should not be mentioned in public is part of the schizophrenic's secondary process. Herr E.'s authorities are 'sick' from the view point of the vacationer in the sense that they do not fully appreciate his needs. If you just fall into being a part of such a system, there is no relativity and the effectiveness of your help from your emotional condition is decreased.

Thus the therapist will constellate resistance if she does not like one of the client's parts, thinks it is sick or tries to change it. No one, not even a part of the personality likes being disliked. Resistance from a part of a personality without a metacommunicator is a more serious resistance than one normally met with in therapy because it is a resistance which cannot be discussed or analyzed. And therapy done in the neighborhood of a resisting part is guaranteed to be only partial. If rapport and relatedness mean understanding and direct contact with all the parts of the personality, then process work may be useful when considering how to deal with an extreme state.

WORKING WITH THE COLLECTIVE

The lack of a metacommunicator and the lack of interest in psychological development make the schizophrenic a poor candidate for normal psychotherapeutic treatment before, during or after an episode. Though there are many people who do want to work with themselves, those who do not are a puzzle to therapists. It could be that one reason for their resistance is for the benefit of the collective: if everything could be solved internally for the individual, there would be no impetus for collective change.

Working with the collective situation might then be a part of the schizophrenic's treatment. In Herr E.'s case, working with the collective would be useful because he is not asking for psychotherapeutic help in the ordinary sense, that is, for growth or insight. His personal problem is not personal if there is no metacommunicator.

Working with the collective means bringing the information channelled by Herr E. to the Swiss collective. By means of radio, television, plays, books and newspapers the larger collective can be informed about different aspects of the conflict between the vacationer and the worker. Switzerland may be faced with having to investigate the consequences of the ancient ideal 'Work and Prayer Make Life Sweet.'

Support for the collective importance of schizophrenia can be found in its demography. Already in 1835, J.C. Prichard (Torrey, 1983, p. 204) said 'Insanity belongs almost exclusively to the civilized races of man: it scarcely exists among savages, and is rare in barbarous countries.' More modern studies (Torrey, 1983, pp. 96, 206) state that 'there is clearly a disproportionate number of schizophrenics who come from the cities, and especially from those portions of cities where the poor live.' Countries like Japan, England, Denmark and Germany have the same rate as the USA. Higher rates are found in the Scandinavian countries, Ireland and Northern Yugoslavia. Lower rates have been found in Africa, with the exception of those exposed to western technology and culture. It is very rare in Papua New Guinea, which is probably the least developed country remaining in the world. Clearly the collective plays a role in schizophrenia and, as in the case of Herr E., we all need to relativize some of our most rigid 'authority' concepts.

Chapter 5
SCHIZOPHRENIA AND ALTERED STATES

Extreme states such as those occurring during schizophrenic episodes are excellent examples of the individuality of processes. They operate very exactly and powerfully and cannot be changed even if an entire city fights against them. They are tightly enclosed systems of patterns and information. If you do not comprehend the exact pattern, you have the feeling that the psychotic process is driven by a mechanical, powerful machine.

These psychotic episodes can be understood with a little reflection. Once the pattern is deciphered, we are able to predict the psychotic's behavior. In fact, understanding the patterns behind a psychotic episode makes the workings of the episode appear mechanical. This may sound inhuman and to some extent it is since the pattern operates without an available observer, without a metacommunicator, cannot be interrupted and is closed to outside intervention, unless the intervention enters the pattern on its own terms. We should also note that there are mechanical patterns in all of us. Our metacommunicator, however, disturbs our patterns so that they are not as apparent as in an extreme state.

HERR B.
Let us see the operation of such patterns in the case of Herr B. I want to describe him from the city's point of view, and then let him speak for himself.

Herr B. was brought to the attention of the social work office because no one knew what to do with him. He sometimes considers himself a healer or enlightened soul and frequently travels to South American countries. Most recently he tried to marry the daughter of one of the heads of government there, made an awful spectacle of himself and was quietly and kindly bound to the chair of a Swissair 747 and sent home. As he got off the plane he ran to a downtown department store and stole a garbage can which he said he needed to urinate into. Next, he was caught stealing the cover to another such can which he said he needed to cover the first one with. Since he was obviously not malicious, the police let him go with warnings only to be called for a third time to arrest him later that day. This time Herr B. was singing too loudly in his apartment late at night. When the police entered the scene they found him sitting in an empty bath tub fully clothed.

The psychiatrist handling this case temporarily controlled the acute episode with psychopharmica and then released him. Now Herr B. appears at the social service station, a man of around fifty years of age, well dressed, somewhat on the heavy side, obviously slowed down by drugs. He looks a bit depressed, sits with his head bent down and with his hands folded politely together on his knees. As I saw him he reacted and related warmly to those around him, but had a funny glint in his eye. His expression was that of someone who has seen something awesome and impressive but cannot speak about it and tries to cover it up with a pleasant, sociable smile.

HERR B. IN PERSON
As we drink coffee together, Herr B. complains about the side effects of the psychopharmica he is using. Then he says, when asked about the book on hypnosis he is carrying with him,

Herr B.:   I want to work with self hypnosis and cybernetics in order to free myself from the psychopharmica which help me to be normal. . . . My problem is that I get into states of the subconscious and do not know what I do.

As he talks I notice that his tempo is slow yet intense. He looks depressed, except in a normal depression themes do not switch back and forth as they do with Herr B. I imagine his behavior must be strongly induced by the drugs. They apparently quiet him down in the foreground, while the background excitement in his life is still shining through.

PROCESS STRUCTURE

I notice first of all that the state he is now in has a metacommunicator because he is able to talk about himself. He talks about other (subconscious) states and is interested in controlling and freeing himself. His primary process is wanting to work with himself and being the victim of the problem of slipping into unconscious states. These states are themselves secondary processes which I will have to find out more about. In the moment, then, he is speaking as a normal person about other states, extreme ones, psychotic ones for which there is no metacommunicator who observes or knows. I wonder if there is a function to not knowing what he is doing in those states.

Arny: Tell me more about hypnosis.
Herr B.:   Hypnosis helps me when things get too objective. Then the world seems sterile and meaningless to me, really, that can be too much, it is dangerous. Then I do not notice that I begin to slide into these states . . . afterwards I notice that the world has caved in, everything is chaotic. No one can talk to me when I am in a chaotic state.
Arny: What do you mean that things get too objective?
Herr B.:   I mean that if I relate to life as if it were really real, then I get lonely and bored, but I must be careful about going too 'subjective,' . . . If I am 100 percent normal then I am unhappy and the world makes me unhappy.

HYPNOSIS

Notice that in the first of his statements presented above he says that hypnosis should replace psychopharmica in making him normal, that is, in keeping him away from 'subconscious states.' Now he says that he wants hypnosis to help him to get away from the normal condition in which things are objective.

If he is too normal, he says he is too objective, and then the world becomes depressing for him, as a result he becomes subjective, introverted, bored and finally flips. If he is too subjective he has to become more objective and normal, but the normal situation is intolerable and so he flips into another world.

At the moment he is using psychopharmica and self hypnosis in two ways. He uses them to do what he has been told they do, namely to help him be 'normal' or 'objective' and not 'chaotic.' And he is using hypnosis and drugs for another purpose which he is less aware of, namely to free himself from the 'objective,' painful world which is intolerable to him. In other words, he is using the same medication which is supposed to make him normal in order to enter into altered states. People sometimes use medication in order to enter altered states though they are simultaneously afraid of being possessed and overwhelmed by these powerful secondary processes. If medication is used against objective, normal life, then despite its normal effects it is bound to contribute, in Herr B.'s situation, to tripping the normal state into another episode at another time.

THE PURPOSE OF NO FEEDBACK LOOP
Since Herr B. claims that he is now objective, his slightly depressed expression is not only due to the drugs, but to his unhappiness about being objectively in this world. Getting jilted by the South American beauty or being turned down by a Swiss girl-friend are probably enough to throw him into unhappiness, which he then apparently deals with by becoming lonely and 'subjective.' This means, I suspect, cutting off feedback from the world around him, so that '. . . no one can talk to me . . .' and he is free to indulge in compensatory fantasies and states. One of his doctors told me that in these states he imagines that he is Jesus.

The usefulness of the secondary process, the so-called

chaotic state, is to cut off the pain of being rejected and to experience the love of God. Here we see one of the important purposes for a missing feedback loop which I discussed in Chapter 3 in connection with Herr E.'s extreme states: not picking up what others are doing and saying is a means of saving yourself from pain and disappointment and experiencing another, lifesaving reality. Picking up other's feedback would disturb the compensatory effect of the other reality and result in a more violent experience of this world.

BECOMING A HYPNOTIST
A hypnotist can control, in Herr B.'s mind at least, the states of consciousness which he is subjected to. Hence, his interest in becoming a hypnotist is similar to the drive to become a psychiatrist or psychologist; one wants to understand and control what happens. If Herr B. does not learn how to do it consciously, then he will unconsciously slip into becoming a healer or a Jesus figure. Thus, in his normal state, the way he is now, he is asking for integration of the experiences he had when he was in a psychotic episode.

THERAPY STRATEGY
If Herr B.'s present primary process is to be objective and normal, his secondary one is to be a healer or hypnotist. When he flips, he becomes the healer, and then his secondary process will be to become objective like the police who pick him up, telling him he should not steal ash cans or sing too loudly in an empty bathtub. If we acted like Jesus when he is in a 'flipped' condition, then he would begin to identify with the 'objective ones,' and look the way he does now.

Process work in the present, normal state means helping him integrate his Jesus/healer figure, as in ordinary psychotherapy in which you talk about the secondary process with a metacommunicator. He said that he would have liked ordinary psychotherapeutic help. I told him that I thought it might be a good idea for him to really study hypnotism and other psychological methods for working with altered states. He was delighted with the idea.

ALTERED STATES AND THE HYPNOTIC PROCESSES

Hypnosis, one of the ancestors of modern psychology, is a method of altering states of consciousness or, rather, for getting around consciousness and accessing unconscious secondary processes. Spontaneous alterations of consciousness (i.e., of the primary process) as they occur in schizophrenia where the secondary process becomes primary and the earlier primary one becomes secondary are natural and meaningful conditions which one frequently finds in psychology and medicine. The following illustrate some examples of various processes which operate in hypnotic-like fashion. Seeing that these states occur in all of us will enable us to gain a greater appreciation for the reversals which occur in schizophrenia.

STOPPING THE WORLD

When the conscious mind is unwilling or unable to let in a secondary process such as the psychic healer or Jesus Christ, then the psyche operates in such a way as to get around consciousness by 'caving the world in,' as Herr B. states. Don Juan, Castaneda's shamanic mentor, would call this phenomenon 'stopping the world,' or, as we would say, inhibiting the determining function of primary processes. Someone who is afraid of the intellect and of thinking, for example, will experience sudden states of logical and sequential opinions or thought. A rigid thinking type will periodically be overwhelmed by sentiment for the world.

THE POWER OF POSITIVE THINKING

Many processes operate in a hypnotic fashion to alter consciousness, but are not explicitly called hypnosis. For example, going to the movies is an effective means of altering consciousness. Talking to yourself with the 'power of positive thinking,' insisting that everything is fine and nothing is wrong is hypnosis. Hypnotism works if the pattern for it is in your dreams, if there is a secondary process in the background waiting to be integrated or to superimpose itself upon the primary one. When hypnotism does not work, it is not due to the lack of power of the hypnotist, but due to a lack of pattern for the hypnosis in the client's secondary process. Thus if a mechanic dreams about God, gets sick and then goes to a priest who advises him to trust in God, his chances of getting better are high because getting well and believing in God are already present in his secondary process. In my experience, if this were not his process, belief alone would work only temporarily because it is not possible to insert a secondary process into someone for more than just a few moments. If a type of behavior is not present in one's secondary process, it will not hold.

CHANNEL BLOCKING
Another way to alter awareness is to switch out of or block the channels in which awareness is operating at any given moment. Thus if you are bothered by imagining (a visual channel experience) terrible things happening in the future, going to the movies will make you feel better because the visual and auditory excitement will temporarily block out your own inner visualizations.

If you are a visual or verbal/auditory type, then feeling your body will give you the experience of an altered state of consciousness. If you are a feeling person, pressing yourself to focus on dream imagery (switching from proprioception to visualization) will create an altered state.

Illness can also alter the state of consciousness. When you get sick with the flu, your temperature goes up and you become sleepy and drowsy. This is an extreme state of proprioception. The flu changed your channels, taking you out of your normal one (most westerners are visual or auditory) and forced you to feel your aches, pains, pressures and temperatures.

EPILEPSY
Channel switching, channel blocking and accessing secondary processes are all methods for causing a change in

awareness. Organic brain changes, psychological shock or epileptic seizures also alter consciousness by switching channels. The difference is that in these examples, unlike the ones above, the person is not in control. A typical statement from a woman who experiences violent 'grand mal' attacks is,

I do not notice until afterwards that an attack is coming. I am simply thrown to the floor and awake later, confused, not knowing where I am, bleeding as if I had scratched my face on something while falling.

This woman is diagnosed as having grand mal epilepsy. From the process viewpoint, however, she has a rigid primary process which does not allow aggression. She is strongly attached to being religiously 'good.' Her unoccupied or most unconscious channel is movement (the unoccupied channel is always where great experiences happen. (See *Working with the Dreaming Body*, Chapter 2.) But since her pious background does not allow her to move much, let alone move aggressively (her kinesthesia is therefore unoccupied), she experiences being 'thrown to the floor,' and being the victim of 'attacks,' both of which happen to her. Thus, aggression and movement are secondary; they are not part of her conscious identity or her primary process.

SUICIDAL FANTASIES

Suicide is yet another method of switching out of one state into another. When someone who does not normally experience extreme 'psychotic' states tells me that she has fantasies of committing suicide, I take that fantasy very seriously and encourage her to do it right then with me.

A woman suffering from a long-standing depression complained that she had had enough of this world and wanted to die. I told her to do it right there with me. She closed her eyes, began to breathe deeply and lay down on the floor. Apparently this was her method of 'dying.' After a few minutes she opened her eyes and told me she had had a vision of standing in front of the gates of heaven. A great voice yelled at her, saying, 'Get the hell out of here. Go back to life and work instead of being so lazy.' I then knew how to work with her depression. Instead of being sympathetic to her sad story about life, I told her to stop being so lazy and get to work. This brought immediate positive feedback from her.

Altered states are full of unlived creativity. I could never have given her that vision or have helped her in any other way. Instead, I had empathized with her and felt badly for her. For her, dying meant altering her state of consciousness, dropping out of her feelings of sadness and heaviness. By breathing deeply, she killed the primary experience of sadness. From a process point of view, suicide means overcoming the primary process. In this woman's case, by breathing deeply, a new message announced itself through vision and voice. Thus alterations of consciousness can be accomplished through accessing secondary processes (like the healer), channel blocking (like the movies), channel changing (like feeling your body if you are a visual type) or suicidal fantasies (like letting your primary process die).

We could enumerate many other methods for spontaneously altering states of consciousness. All of us use such methods consciously or unconsciously every day. A therapist with knowledge of these patterns and methods will be able to help her client go through such processes more consciously and usefully.

FLIPPING
The last program I want to mention is the one which happens most frequently in schizophrenia: exchanging the primary process (like the victim) for the secondary process (like Jesus, the healer), dropping the metacommunicator who, like most censors, may be too rigid to let this altered state happen, and experiencing what the outside world calls a 'psychotic episode.' This flip has much in common with the processes of suicidal fantasies, channel blocking, channel switching and accessing secondary processes.

Why nature prefers one method over another will be

discussed in the next chapter. For the moment, we need to remember that the same process of flipping which creates the episode is the process which can reverse it, and that one of the many functions of flipping is to avoid pain and to allow secondary processes to come up. We need to remember that belonging to the 'grower's club' means suffering the conflict between the primary and secondary processes and experiencing the pain and conflict which happens when the one begins to transform the other. Nature has provided us with many organic methods of avoiding pain and confrontations between the primary and secondary systems. If we do not learn to follow these processes, then nature does it for us by producing experiences such as schizophrenia and epilepsy. We see how these may be avoided in certain cases through following the individual processes of pain avoidance with expertise and appreciation.

HERR B.'s FEEDBACK

For Herr B., avoiding pain was an important process. Thinking of accessing the hypnotic effects of the healer in the background, I said quite simply to him,

Arny: Let's stop talking about all of these painful past experiences, and try to get you a job where you will have a lot of fun and can look positively towards the future.

Herr B.: I have experienced this sitting with you people very positively. One hundred times better than in the psychiatric clinic where one is always asked and troubled with 'How are you feeling?' Here, we had a good time . . . part of my disease is being able to relate to others. I cannot go into a cafe and talk normally to people. This helped me!

Two days later, Herr B. came back to us looking very happy, clean-shaven and full of warmth.

Herr B.: I owe you my health. Self hypnosis helps the patients. We need to work and watch our thoughts. . . . I should have used it earlier . . . all psychically ill people are unconscious. You do not know what you have done for humanity. I owe you a lot. I will make notes about what I could do for you.

He identifies himself at this moment as a patient and member of the 'grower's club' by saying, 'I owe you a lot.' He simultaneously experiences beginning the training to be a healer when he says, 'I will make notes about what I could do for you.' These statements give me hope for the future. From his present viewpoint, he will begin to study psychology. I can imagine, however, the possibility of another episode in the near future from his sentence, 'All psychically ill people are unconscious,' implying the possibility that they will need to be awakened.

Continuing to work with Herr B. would mean literally helping him to take notes so that he could help not only himself and me but others as well. If he were to become his total self, the chances are that he would continue his interest in psychology by studying it. No doubt the fate of many people who have experienced extreme states is to become psychologists in the future.

Chapter 6
PROCESSING A CATATONIC STATE

Patricia suffers from a catatonic form of schizophrenia. She assumes a rigid posture and is almost mute or stuporous for long periods. She is led by hand into the social work station by a psychologist. In fact, she looks like a little girl passively following her mother. I am quickly informed that she is twenty-two, has been a brilliant student in the Swiss schools but has become increasingly withdrawn and dreamy over the years. There is apparently no organic brain trouble. The social worker caring for Patricia says that Patricia has always been very polite but since she has left school, she irritates everyone who tries to help her by being listless and passive. I am told that she will not answer questions when they are asked.

Patricia is sitting next to me now in the circle. I sit to her immediate right, her social worker sits to her left. Joe and two other social workers are also present. Patricia has an unconvincing smile on her face, superimposed upon a listless facial expression which becomes even more vacant whenever she is not being addressed. When asked a question, she will look at the questioner for a moment, smile and then stare blankly and vacantly into space. A typical interaction happens right at the beginning of the interview. Ruth, the social worker handling Patricia's case, talks rapidly about the passivity of her client as if Patricia were not there.

Ruth: Patricia's mother came with her once and told her how to behave. Her mother said, 'Say hello to everyone and say goodbye, be a nice girl Patricia.'

Ruth now looks at Patricia, apparently for a response, but Patricia just sits rigidly and stares into space, giving no overt reaction.

Jan (another social worker):   Patricia, did you get angry at your mother?

Patricia still looks blank, but then with a quick and sudden movement, as if realizing she had been asked a question, whispers in a barely audible tone of voice:

Patricia: I am not so little . . . any more . . . and my mother does not realize this. On the other hand my mother wants to be helpful, she realizes that I am very afraid. . . .

Patricia puts her hand in front of her mouth and pauses.

Ruth (with irritation):   Patricia, I think you are really blocked, and I want to help you work out your problems.

Patricia just looks down and does not answer: in fact, she hardly blinks.

UNDERSTANDING PATRICIA
Before we examine Patricia's process, I recommend that we perform a technical exercise in order that we understand her behavior. In fact, I strongly recommend to anyone working with extreme states to act out the client's signals as a way of understanding her.

In order to understand and appreciate the usefulness of Patricia's state, try sitting a bit hunched forward, smile nicely, act stuporous and blank, a little slowed down and drugged, as if you are just waking up in the morning. Now ask someone to bother you with questions, or try to remember what it is like to have someone else ask you questions. After a long pause, answer with one word reactions. Then sink back again out of visual and verbal contact. What do you experience?

After doing this exercise, one of my classes told me that they did not feel psychotic in this state, but more interested in maintaining their own inner world. They unanimously agreed that in such a state they did not want to be disturbed or pressed by questions. Most felt that they were too weak and passive to tell the questioner to be quiet and leave them alone. Therefore they could only smile sweetly and drop out of contact.

THOUGHT BLOCKING AND BEING CONTROLLED
Like many people suffering from the subtype of schizophrenia called catatonia, Patricia complains about difficulty in concentrating and says that she is disturbed by the camera, for example, which 'controls my behavior.' Nevertheless she does not object to the presence of the camera and even jokes about it a bit when given the opportunity.

Patricia says that her thoughts are totally controlled or, as termed in psychiatry, blocked. The experience of being controlled by the camera, together with blocking, the gradual sliding away from social contact and the lack of commitment to her school and work are symptoms connected with the possible diagnosis of schizophrenia.

The individual just on the verge of a catatonic episode emits double signals due to the presence of a metacommunicator. This is in contrast to someone in an extreme state in which signals occur one after the other and not necessarily simultaneously. Therefore, at this point in her life, Patricia has a metacommunicator, albeit a weak one, and thus acts sweetly while sending out negative signals. This makes her seem 'negativistic' and she is often experienced by others as irritating and unresponsive. It is this signal of unresponsiveness that Ruth reacts to aggressively.

PROCESS STRUCTURE

Patricia says she is scared, weak and afraid of life, like a child. The terrified child is her primary process. Her secondary process is experienced as something which 'controls her,' as something which is 'terrifying' and also as the mother who does not realize that she is no longer little. Her secondary process is, pictorially speaking, a mother who controls behavior.

When there is a metacommunicator present, secondary processes come out as double signals filtered through the uniformity of the primary process. When there is no metacommunicator, as in the case of Herr E.'s extreme state, secondary processes follow primary ones sequentially or in a seemingly congruent fashion without disturbing the otherwise uniform primary one. In the case of Herr B., the signal of his secondary process, the split off religious experience, appeared through his depressed primary process as a wild gleam in his eye. In the case of Patricia, her secondary process, the controlling mother, appears through the non-response signal. No response to a stimulus is a negative response, what we call negative feedback. There is no such thing as no communication! Smiling politely is a primary process and no verbal response is a negative signal which controls the entire communicative setting. Hence, the signals which irritate the social workers are controlling signals, Patricia's secondary process, her mother.

STRATEGY

Our work will be aimed at bringing up the controlling power of the mother in such a way that it can be made available to the weak and scared child in the primary process. Aggression and power will not be easy to access because of the weak identity in the primary process. If we cannot access them, then Patricia will very likely continue to be possessed by her lack of responsiveness.

It is important to analyze the process structure of such a client because otherwise one will be unconsciously drawn to combat the mother, either the inner, controlling one or the outer one in order to save the poor child. The weak metacommunicator and extreme lack of response organizes and polarizes those in the environment who become angry at the client for her negativistic attitude. Every attempt to talk to someone who smiles without immediately responding is a useless intervention into a powerful, unchanging process.

The question remains as to how one can communicate directly with a powerful, controlling and apparently nonverbal secondary process. One way is to assume that the process is mother-like, intelligent, capable of taking care of Patricia and independent. It is also necessary to assume that responses need not be verbal, but may be transmitted through signals occurring synchronistically in the environment and physically in the client. After having determined this process structure, I decided to attempt direct communication with Patricia's silence, with what I assumed to be her mother.

Arny: Patricia, I see you go off internally, thinking and quietly meditating while we speak to you. And now, I want you to do this, to follow your own process in great detail. Take a lot of time, and when you are ready, if you want to answer the following questions, answer them. My first question is, do you have any questions of us now?

Patricia begins to go into one of her long pauses. I talk to the others present in order that they do not disturb Patricia's concentration by asking more questions.

Arny: You see, Patricia is now going through an internal process in order to answer my questions in her own time and way.

I notice that Patricia looked down, rotated her eyes slowly in a circle, quickly looked to the left where Ruth was sitting and then swallowed. From body work I have noticed that swallowing is almost always associated with a moment of understanding. Therefore I asked:

Arny: What did you just think?
Patricia (answering immediately):   What should I do for a
    profession?

I was surprised that this intervention worked so well with
an otherwise silent person. This was the first time she posed
a question on her own or said anything directly and without
hesitation. I realized that her answer was positive feedback
to the new exchange method. I repeated her question:

Arny: What profession is the right one for you?

Again filling in the pause to keep the others out of Patricia's
internal process:

Arny: I know you are the only one who can tell us this,
    Patricia, and I trust you to take all the time you
    need, even more than that until you know the
    answer.

Patricia rotated her eyes again, then, after about a minute,
swallowed.
Arny: Yes?
Patricia (immediately):   I want to become a gardener.
Arny: How will you become a gardener?
Patricia (this time responding without using the long pause
    or internal program):   By slowly learning the pro-
    fession, at first part time, living where I am
    presently staying in the moment, then at a later
    time, moving out, working more, beginning to risk
    working and taking chances.

EVALUATION

Once the details of Patricia's internal state are understood it
is possible to access it. She is now speaking like a protective
mother and caring for herself. Therapy at this point would
entail getting her to take a minimal risk right now, as she
suggests, or telling her that she has been courageous to have
risked sharing her ideas with all these 'adults' present.

Continued work would involve a careful communication process in which the therapist attempts to befriend the mothering process and not fight against its controlling negativism.

One advantage of process oriented work is its emphasis upon the nature of individual communication. This means, however, that the therapist must pick up signals which are normally neglected, like swallowing, and must drop her own preferred, usually verbal method of communication. The necessity for greater receptivity to individual communicative modes challenges the way in which one is working and brings more discovery and research to traditional therapeutic methods.

NONVERBAL COMMUNICATION IN EVERYDAY LIFE
The concept that the states met with in psychotic episodes are extreme is due in part to the fact that we are not aware of their appearance in everyday life because they are hidden by a metacommunicator or a strong primary process. Nevertheless they are present. In closing, I want to mention a few of the many nonverbal states we frequently encounter in psychotherapy.

NONVERBAL SECONDARY PROCESSES
1 During ordinary psychotherapy the client goes internal when he is feeling something deeply and is not interested in the conversation. He usually stops talking, looks down at the floor and seems lost in reverie. This emotion requires respect from the therapist by focusing upon proprioceptive (i.e., feeling) experiences or upon memories without requiring the client to 'come back' and communicate to the therapist.

2 When a patient has become comatose because of an accident or near-death condition, the color of the skin, heart rate, breathing rate and pupil dilation are some of many signals which may be used to communicate with.

3 In organic brain disease such as one sees in advanced alcoholism, drug abuse or senility where there is

memory loss, clouding of consciousness or drunken-like behavior, the normal primary process is missing and nonverbal feedback is essential for communication. More will be said about such processes in the chapters on alcohol and heroin addiction.

4 Individuals who are in meditation, in out-of-the-body experiences and near death require nonverbal communication. It is useful to pay attention to the rate at which the eyelids flutter and verbally to guess at the nonverbal feedback about the visions or experiences which may be occurring. (See *Inner Dreambody Work*.)

5 In relationship work, being able to comprehend and work with nonverbal signals can often facilitate the end of a long-standing crisis. (See *the Dreambody in Relationships*.)

Working with extreme states forces us to consider the importance of nonverbal processes. The more we know about them, the better we can deal with people in altered states of consciousness and reduce the loneliness and occasionally catastrophic consequences associated with them by integrating them into ordinary everyday life. Appreciating nonverbal signals and introverted behavior in others and in ourselves enables us to direct our lives from the panoramic viewpoint of dreams and individuation.

Chapter 7
PATTERNS IN SCHIZOPHRENIA

In this chapter ways of working with some commonly occurring verbal and nonverbal communication patterns in schizophrenia are considered. Teaching and training experience indicate that the more familiar a student is with these patterns the easier it is to process them without reference to psychopharmica. Therefore I am going to review some of the patterns which appeared in the last chapters before going on to bipolar disorders.

Torrey (1983) writes that 'when one listens to persons with schizophrenia describe what they experience and observes their behavior, certain abnormalities can be noted.' The following are some of these 'abnormalities,' followed by what I believe are meaningful connections implicit within them.

1 Alterations of the senses
2 Inability to sort and synthesize incoming sensations, and inability therefore to respond appropriately
3 Delusions and hallucinations
4 Altered sense of self
5 Changes in emotions or affects
6 Changes in behavior

Each of these characteristics alone is insufficient evidence to diagnose schizophrenia; the diagnosis depends upon the sum of all the symptoms, not just one alone. Let us look at these characteristics, one by one.

1 ALTERATIONS OF THE SENSES

This refers primarily to amplifications or 'blunting' of channel phenomena. Torrey (1983, p. 7) quotes the protagonist in 'The Tell-Tale Heart' by Edgar Allen Poe:

A   True nervous very, very dreadfully nervous I had been and am! But why will you say that I am mad? The disease had sharpened my senses not destroyed not dulled them. Above all was the sense of hearing acute. I heard things in the heavens and in the earth.

Another schizophrenic described the state in this way:

B   During the last while back I have noticed that noises all seem to be louder to me than they were before. It's as if someone had turned up the volume.

Not only is hearing more acute, but other senses as well:

C   I seem to be noticing colors more than before, although I am not artistically minded.

Other examples of heightened channel experiences include:

D   Everything seems to grip my attention although I am not particularly interested in anything. I am speaking to you just now, but I can hear noises going on next door and in the corridor.

E   If I am talking to someone they only need to cross their legs or scratch their head and I am distracted and forget what I was saying.

F   All sorts of 'thoughts' seem to come to me, as if someone is 'speaking' them inside my head.

Amplifying channels is the basis of process oriented meditation, it is found in Buddhist meditation methods and is the essential element in becoming conscious and aware. In schizophrenia, becoming conscious or aware is a secondary process since it happens autonomously. Channel awareness, increased brightness, distracting sounds, movements, etc. arise spontaneously as if consciousness itself were trying to happen, but the primary process or one's normal attention is not trained to pick it up. The process paradigm does not consider a symptom something to overcome, but an aspect of the personality in need of integration. Thus the therapist could work with these autonomous channel and sensory experiences by encouraging the patient to go more deeply into them. For example, the therapist could recommend in A (above), that the client listen closely to all those noises in heaven and earth and note exactly what they say; in B, that the client talk to the person who has turned up the volume and ask him why he has done that. Could it be that he had not wanted to listen in the past? In C, that the client paint the visual experiences, noting all the colors in detail; in D, that the client listen closely to all the voices around him. The therapist can support the client's disinterest in the conversation by saying. 'You must have noticed that our conversation is not the important thing, there is a lot of superficiality in it. Listen closely to the corridor, make a meditation out of it and tell me exactly what you hear. Then we will find out why you must hear it.' In E, that the client need not concentrate on superficial things, but should feel free and strong to direct the conversation in the way he needs. In F, that the patient find out who is talking inside his head, could it be someone who has a lot of important information for him?

Blunting
Whereas amplification is an early symptom, blunting or deadening of the senses is frequently associated with later stages of schizophrenia.

However hard I looked it was as if I was looking through a daydream and the mass of detail, such as the pattern on a carpet, became lost. (Torrey, 1983, p. 13)

This is visual blunting. Early textbooks on schizophrenia describe proprioceptive blunting or blocking in cases of appendectomies and similar procedures performed with little or no anesthesia. Nurses and other personnel in mental hospitals know very well the phenomenon of schizophrenic patients sustaining injuries such as fractured bones without being in any pain. And, of course, it is quite a common occurrence that schizophrenics will smoke their cigarettes to the end and burn their fingers without realizing it.

According to Torrey, blunting may be related to changes in the limbic area of the lower portion of the brain. Such experiences are, however, also typical of channel changes and are a regular feature of the switch between primary and secondary processes which occur even in ordinary stages of development. The primary process always experiences itself as the victim in pain, but after switching into the secondary process, as in the later stages of schizophrenia as well as in ordinary development where one temporarily takes over a secondary process, the client becomes identified with the secondary process. The secondary process is not the victim of pain, but the agent or pain-maker; hence the client feels no pain – she herself has become a pain-maker. The next step with a schizophrenic patient who feels no pain is to ask why she needs to hurt herself or others.

Another possibility is to ask her if she is having an out-of-the-body experience. It might be useful for the client no longer to have a body; she may need to get rid of the old body in order to change personalities!

2 INABILITY TO SYNTHESIZE AND RESPOND
Torrey (1983, p. 15ff) reports the following excerpts from patients all describing their inability to synthesize and sort incoming perceptions:

> H   I have to put things together in my head. If I look at my watch I see the watchstrap, watch, face, hands and so on, then I have got to put them together to get it into one piece.

I   Everything is in bits. You put the picture up bit by bit into your head. It's like a photograph that's torn in bits and put together again. If you move it's frightening.

J   I can't concentrate on television because I can't watch the screen and listen to what is being said at the same time.

K   If I do something like going for a drink of water, I've got to go over each detail – find cup, walk over, turn tap, fill cup, turn tap off, drink it.

In these cases, we are again dealing with a spontaneous and autonomous increase in awareness. Awareness is being increased without the patient being able to identify with the changes. These experiences are strongly reminiscent of vipassana meditation. An interesting way to work with and amplify these experiences would be to criticize the patient for his past unconsciousness and encourage him to be more meditative and detailed in his method of observing what goes on around him. For example you might say, 'You have been too sloppy with your observations until now and have not noticed enough details. You should be able to notice the way and rate you are breathing, the kinds of feelings you had when your eyes moved to the left and where those feelings originated in your body. Why do you skip over so many details about yourself?'

In the specific cases above you might say the following. In H, 'You should begin to notice the kinds of words people use. How do I use my verbs? What channel am I in now?' In I, 'You need to learn how to put things together. Let me tell you a few bits of a case like yours and you tell me what kind of person it is.' In J, 'Do not move an inch, but concentrate on the following puzzle and put it together. A man. Twenty years old. Has been withdrawing for eight months. Lost his girl-friend. A blond. Why?' (One of my clients answered this question, 'Because this man was not made for this world, he was a fallen star who had lost its way and someone needed to tell his story in a book.') In J, 'Stop trying to do two things at the same time. Do not look but listen to me. Listen only and do not look. Listen to my tone of voice. And when you have registered that, then look and tell me frankly if I look the same as I sound.' In K, 'You are a gifted vipassana meditator. Now let us practice this in eating. First, notice taking the spoon. Now bring the spoon to the mouth. Now open the mouth. Now taste the flavors, salt, sugar. Swallowing. Notice your stomach.'

3 DELUSIONS AND HALLUCINATIONS

I discussed the function of delusions and paranoid beliefs earlier. The persecutor is a part of the personality, a secondary process which the individual finally becomes. The different delusions, whether one is being watched, persecuted or attacked, or whether one is Jesus Christ, the Virgin Mary or the President are all similar experiences in that they are all secondary processes which need to be worked with and integrated.

4 ALTERED SENSE OF SELF

I saw myself in different bodies . . . the night nurse came in and sat under the shaded lamp in the quiet ward. I recognized her as me, and I watched for some time quite fascinated; I had never had an outside view of myself before. In the morning several of the patients having breakfast were me. (Torrey, 1983, p. 34)

I get shaky in the knees and my chest is like a mountain in front of me, and my body actions are different. The arms and legs are apart and away from me and they go on their own. That's when I feel I am the other person and copy their movements, or else stop and stand like a statue. (Torrey, 1983, p. 34).

In the first situation I might recommend to the client to get an outside view of himself or to look at himself in the mirror. I would ask him not only what he sees in the mirror, but what it is like to be the people he dreamed about the night before, or the nurse or the people at the breakfast table. The client needs to know a lot more about other people; he should not just identify unconsciously with them, but should feel them and know them more intimately and find out why these people are all inside him. What do they have in common? This client has a big need to know more about himself and has not gone far enough with his own processes until now.

In the second situation, I would recommend to the client that she move in ways she has not done before. Since movements and feelings are happening spontaneously to her, I would suggest that she take it over by standing up with me right in the moment and experimenting with the movements her body is trying to make. This could be a lot of fun; maybe a story will come out, or perhaps she will become a statue. Out of the body movements will come a meaningful dance or posture that could be worked with creatively.

5 CHANGES IN EMOTIONS OR AFFECTS
Connected with this euphoric state, I experienced a gentle sensation of warmth over my whole body, particularly on my back, and a sensation of my body having lost its weight and gently floating. (Torrey, 1983, p. 36)

What are the possible ways of working with this state? Since it is indicative of a strong proprioceptive experience, one might try amplifying it through yoga to increase the awareness of the proprioception and then find the meaning of these experiences for the client's everyday life. I did this recently with one of my clients and he told me I was crazy. I said, 'Don't mind me, just do the Yoga.' While in the midst of one asana, he began screaming, 'Oh . . . oh . . . God . . . God. . . .' I told him to quieten down long enough to tell me what God was doing. 'GET TO WORK YOU LAZY BASTARD' was what God had said to him. So I said this to the client too and he left quite soberly, saying, 'Let's wait for the next session.'

6 CHANGES IN BEHAVIOR

Withdrawing, remaining quietly in one place for long periods, being agitated and immobility are all common behavioral 'disorders' of this illness. (Torrey, 1983 p. 39ff)

> When I am walking along the street it comes on me. I start to think deeply and I start to go into a sort of trance. I think so deeply that I almost get out of this world. Then you get frightened that you are going to get into a jam and lose yourself.

> The state of indifference reigning until now was abruptly replaced by inner and outer agitation. At first I felt obliged to get up and walk; it was impossible to stay in bed. Singing a requiem without pause, I marched three steps forward and three steps back, an automatism that wearied me exceedingly and which I wished someone would help me break. I could not do it alone, for I felt forced to make these steps and if I stopped from exhaustion, even for a moment, I felt guilty again.

> . . . I was to lean on the back of my head and on my feet in bed, and twist my neck by throwing my body with a jerk from side to side. I fancy that I never attempted this with sincerity, because I feared to break my neck.

In the second instance, I would say, 'You poor person. You really need someone to enter with you into that lonely world, so I am going to do that and I promise to stay there with you until the terrible witch-like spell upon you breaks. I love marching and singing. Now, let us get up and march together, one, two, three, one, two, three, and let us sing together . . . by the way, what is the meaning of this requiem and for whom was it sung? How interesting. One, two, three, do not forget the steps. Let's keep going, for if we stop too early we are guilty of not really fulfilling a part of your myth. Only when it is completed can we both be free. I really understand you, you know, because I too often

feel driven to do things, even though I hate doing them.'
In this case, there is no choice about breaking the spell
alone. The man cannot break this spell, so it would be
unwise to advise it. As far as we can see, there is no pattern
for that, so it will not work. The man needs relationship
with an outer person and asks for that.
In the other case, however, the pattern is a bit different.
The patient says that he tried to resist the spell. Therefore I
would say, 'Wow, you are lucky, you have a really powerful
taskmaster inside. I am glad you did not break your neck
and follow him, that shows that you are stronger than he is
and have more feeling than he does. But I wonder, what can
we do with that force? How could you apply that discipline
in your life? Have you finished high school? Are you afraid
to finish college? Can you hold down a job?'

OPEN QUESTIONS ABOUT SCHIZOPHRENIA

It is frequently asked why schizophrenia often occurs early
in life and why its onset is frequently connected with taking
drugs. One answer to both of these questions from my
practice is that most episodes seem to be an attempt to open
the young person's mind to secondary material which has
been forbidden by his environment. Schizophrenia among
young people often looks like an attempt to broaden the
mind.

For example, a family came to see me with their son and
complained that the son had lost his interest in going into
the father's business after a psychotic episode induced by
ingesting hallucinogenic drugs in India during his travels
there. They brought him in to my office and he said to me
that he was no longer himself.

He: I was Peter, Allan, John, Alex, I was the universe, I
came from all over, but I was not from this country I
really come from, from Spain.
Me: Was it enjoyable not to be yourself?
He: No, I did not like it. I wandered the streets and had
nothing to eat.
Me: How did you get back into yourself?

He: After months of people asking me who I was I decided I had to become myself again.

Me: And what were you like before you went to India, what did it do for you?

He: I had a narrow mind before. I saw only one goal, and that was to become a famous businessman. Now, I have other goals, many, and they are connected with the relationship to God and the desire to know myself.

Me: Have you had any dreams recently?

He: I dreamed that I was high up on a mountain, and looking down I saw little people, and a river running through the valleys.

At this point, he got up on one leg, stood up as if on a mountain and looked down upon me in a strange way. He no longer saw or heard me and I realized that he was in an altered state. The best way to help him through the state, I thought, would be to get into it with him. So I got up on the mountain with him.

Me: I want to come up with you on the mountain. Hi there. Nice up here. What shall we do now? How do we get down?

He: Talk to God.

Me: I like that. God, what would you suggest to my friend?

My patient began to act in the role of God and said:

He (acting God): He must work hard on himself, and get to know other human beings, and learn to face me, man to God.

Then he turned to me as the patient and asked:

He: What should I do with my life?

Me: Study yourself. Study psychology and begin to learn about God and how to be with him.

He: Exactly. Thanks. I do not like many of the people my age because they have such weak and narrow goals.

REVERSAL OF PROCESS STRUCTURE

Schizophrenia is one of the many types of psychoses in which the primary process of the individual – which is originally adapted to the culture in which she is living – is exchanged for a secondary process. This gives rise to the appearance of a total personality change. The emerging 'personality,' that is, the new primary process, is often perceived as having nothing in common with the earlier personality. It is this total personality change which is termed 'psychosis.' In process terms the primary and secondary processes of an individual reverse.

The young man above became the whole universe, in part because his primary goal was to become a businessman. If you remember, Herr E. was previously a hard worker with a secondary interest in relaxing, now he is a relaxer during the period of life when most people are in the midst of working hard. His secondary process is described as the authorities of the world.

Herr B. is a rather intelligent, academic and well-adapted fellow, with a slight depression and secondary interests in healing and hypnotism when he is in his 'normal condition,' and is Jesus Christ when he is flipped. The woman mentioned in the chapter on Herr B. is the Virgin Mary with secondary and projected negative mother characteristics in her flipped phase, and is a negative mother with no interest in God, healing or love when she is 'normal.'

Patricia was originally a highly intelligent and successful child with a bit of a dreamy nature when she was younger, and now she is a totally dreamy, terrified person whose secondary process is intelligent and motherly.

SCHIZOPHRENIA AND THE COLLECTIVE

Herr E. is the relaxer at Switzerland's Round Table. Herr B., the one who wants to avoid pain, becomes Jesus and, together with the woman who calls herself the Virgin Mary in an extreme state, balances the world's lack of belief in the reality of the gods.

All of these people are not quietly schizophrenic. They

disturb the city because their secondary processes are unconscious phenomena for most of us. Herr E. upsets the police with his letters, Herr B. has to be captured and sent home from a South American country and Patricia upsets everyone around her by doing absolutely nothing. In other words, these people belong to given systems and societies.

THE NATURE OF THE PSYCHOTIC PRIMARY PROCESS

The primary process during the psychotic episode compensates a given cultural viewpoint. The constant 1 percent of the world's population suffering from schizophrenia tempts me to make the following hypothesis. In a given collective, the schizophrenic patient occupies the part of the system in a family and culture which is not taken up by anyone else. She occupies the unoccupied seat at the Round Table, so to speak, in order to have every seat filled. She is the collective's dream, their compensation, secondary process and irritation.

An Example

I recall Lilly, a very delicate catatonic young woman of about eighteen years who felt like a goddess. She did not talk and was so sensitive that the slightest sound made her cry. She had to pray for the animals and people of this world day and night. When I saw her together with her family, they complained that earlier she was good in school and not so overly sensitive.

The father informed me that he had occasional heart attacks, and said, 'I have been told that they could be a matter of life and death, but do not think that I would spoil myself at this point by treating myself as if I were sensitive, frail or something special!' The mother and brother nodded in support of the father's attitude, Lilly is obviously their dream.

METACOMMUNICATORS

Since a schizophrenic has no metacommunicator with whom we can discuss the different processes occurring, there is, during the episode at least, no one present in the patient who believes that he is ill. The given culture which is disturbed by the activities of the patient defines the patient as being ill. This cultural attitude towards schizophrenia was mirrored in the original psychoanalytical dream theories which viewed dreams in part as pathological material.

Herr E. thinks the authorities are ill, not he. Herr B., when he is normal, considers himself ill, otherwise he is a manic healer. Patricia says she needs a profession, but does not complain about being ill. In the opinion of the schizophrenic while in the extreme state, it is the primary process of the culture which is not well; it is our consciousness, our minds which are not in order.

THE SURPRISE FUNCTION
The schizophrenic surprises and shocks his environment because of the sudden emergence of a new personality. As secondary processes arise in place of primary ones, without the facilitation of a metacommunicator, what used to be John is now the Devil, Napoleon, Jesus Christ or some other surprising figure.

A therapist cannot claim to know her client if she cannot imagine what the client will look like in a flipped state. In order to do this, the therapist must be able to pick up the client's secondary process in the moment they are together and sharpen her perception and senses. If she is successful at this, there should be no surprises and no malpractice suits.

For example, Alice is a sweet and beautiful woman of twenty-three. When I asked her how she was, she smiled warmly and looked at me but her eyes were a bit vacant. When I recommended to her to look vacant, she giggled and then paused without apparently doing anything. Her vacancy was a secondary tendency to leave the situation. I asked her if she had ever tried to leave this world by committing suicide. She told me about many near-death experiences she had had with drugs, and then told me the story of her attempted suicide. After having had a lovely afternoon with her therapist and a fine dinner with some friends, they were shocked and surprised to find her lying on the floor of her room the next morning, unable to awaken because of an overdose of sleeping pills.

Alice's friends and therapist did not pick up the signals of her secondary process which was to leave this world, NOW. Behind her sweet and adapted expression was a double signal representing that part of her which was not here and did not want to be here. When she actually tried to leave, her friends were shocked, not having been aware of her earlier signals. Alice might be classified as being in the beginning stages of schizophrenia. She wants to leave this world because she is not interested in it or herself and appears to dislike talking about herself much.

SIGNALS IN DREAM AND BODYWORK

This tendency to leave is apparent in her dreams as well. In one dream, Alice saw fire and ran to save herself. She went straight to a cemetery but, noticing that the fire was coming there too, pressed her lips together and had the magical effect of putting out the fire.

When working with her on the dream, I resisted the motion of one of her hands at one point. At first she went blank and said she did not want to get angry. Then she began to get really angry, wanting to fight and explode with anger. After a little wrestling, she abruptly sat down with a happy expression on her face and said she loved wrestling but that she was angry at her parents for many things but was afraid to tell them so.

If we connect her body signals and dream together we can see that she first gets angry (i.e., to be on fire) and then represses her anger, as seen in the dream by running from the fire to the cemetery and in her signals by looking vacant. She identifies herself as a good daughter living at home and being thankful to her parents who direct her life. Her blankness is going to a cemetery, dying, so to speak, instead of being angry. When I asked her to tell me what happens when she presses her lips together as in the dream, she did it and said it meant 'talking, being angry.' She then stated, 'I would rather die than be angry at someone whom I do not like,' whereupon she began once again to vocalize her grievances against her parents.

Alice shows us that suicide, blanking out or flipping into a 'surprising' secondary state is a stage in the midst of a process which consists of getting angry, not wanting to be angry, acting blankly and then finally expressing the anger. Knowing the pattern behind such processes allows us to help their messages and meanings unfold in a more useful way for the individual and the world than suicide or insanity.

THE BEGINNER'S MIND

Why do we tend to either miss or underrate signals which are, a priori, as obvious as other signals? One reason for our oversight and inability to pick up certain messages is insufficient education in signal theory. Another reason is our unconscious tendency to complete, harmonize, perfect or idealize the unknown. We can see this demonstrated in the well-known example in figure 7.1. If ten people look at the circle below, only one in ten will notice that there is a gap in an otherwise circular line. The rest will see only the circle itself.

Figure 7.1 Circular figure with point missing in lower left quadrant

Analogously, when we see a beautiful, youthful person with a winning smile, few are likely to think that a fleeting though repetitive signal such as a blank or vacant expression could be of much significance.

Thus one of the challenges in working with extreme and borderline states is to examine critically our tendency to overlook disharmonious signals. Missing signals of discontent allows us to idealize the efficacy of our methods. A positive way of formulating this challenge is to understand borderline states as tests in developing what Suzuki (1976) calls in his book on Zen, a 'beginner's mind.'

Having a beginner's mind is the only way to help the therapist work with extreme states, for it allows a more developed perception of the environment and a more developed feedback loop, the two things the person suffering from schizophrenia lacks. The beginner's mind neither thinks nor feels, but is simply open. A beginner's mind notices that the schizophrenic in the extreme state seems unrelated to his immediate environment, flip-flops according to who occupies what part in his field and sends valuable nonverbal messages to the rest of us which need to be taken seriously.

Part III
MANIA AND DEPRESSION

Chapter 8
DEPRESSION AND SUICIDE

Manic-depressive illness, now referred to as bipolar disorder by DSM III, is, in its classical form, easy to differentiate from schizophrenia. The clinical picture of the bipolar disorder is dominated by congruency between the individual's mood (either elevated or depressed) and the delusions or hallucinations which coincide with the mood. A schizophrenic can be God and continue eating dinner, whereas a person in a manic phase will feel like a savior, act like a savior and be euphorically helpful. Bipolar disorders are frequently found in higher social economic groups, whereas schizophrenia, in the United States at least, is a disturbance commonly associated with lower income families. The manic person has less need for sleep, is very active, talkative, displays rapid thinking and short attention and is often inflated in self value. The depressed phase of the disorder is characterized by feeling empty, sad and irritable, sleeping too little or too much, having a poor appetite and losing interest in ordinary life. People with bipolar disorders have periodic episodes of mania or depression. In Western Europe, I think at the present time we see mostly the depressed side of the so-called bipolar disorder.

Frau R. would probably be diagnosed as having a psychotic depression. She has been an irritating and difficult problem for the social service people for the past year, since her first visit after having tried to commit suicide. She still feels severely depressed and wants to die.

I want to point out, however, that she comes for help but

does not present depression as her main problem. She comes for help because she lost her false teeth at the bottom of the Lake of Zurich after an attempt to drown herself. She was fished out of the lake by the city police. This suicide attempt not only left her without her teeth (the ostensible reason for coming to the social service station), but without any further interest in living. Her present depression began about three years ago when she was fired from her job at a candy store because she lost the use of one of her hands in an accident.

She enters the interview room, about fifty-five years of age, ashen colored and heavy set, moving and talking very slowly, as if she were dragging one hundred years of misery behind her. After a few minutes of polite chatter I ask her about her most recent suicide attempt and she answers,

Frau R.:   I tried to jump into the water but was not suc-
           cessful. There I lost my teeth, watch and glasses
           . . . the police only found my watch and glasses.
           That was a serious loss for me. Life no longer
           gives me any pleasure . . . if I had good teeth and
           my old job back, then I would enjoy myself.

In transcribing the tape I notice that I missed her logical manner, her matter-of-fact attitude. She is telling a sad story without being overtly sad. I did not notice this consciously, but began unconsciously to take over the sadness and fight the matter-of-fact attitude.

Arny: If I were in your situation and was feeling so badly,
        feeling as if life no longer gave me any pleasure,
        what would you advise me?
Frau R.:   I could not help. Psychiatric help stinks anyhow. I
           hate talking . . . why would you have the feeling
           you should help me anyhow? I do not expect it.
Arny: Would you then like to commit suicide again?
Frau R.:   Yes.
She moves forward to get some tea from the table in front of her.

Social Worker: I feel helpless and hopeless with you.
Frau R.:   I do not expect help from you.

PROCESS STRUCTURE
Her primary process is to be suicidal: 'I tried to jump into
the water.' She identifies herself primarily as an old woman
who is the victim of aging, as seen in the statement. 'I lost
my teeth, watch and glasses.' She does not want help and
hates her helpers.

Her secondary process can be seen in the statement: 'Life
no longer gives me any pleasure.' Her secondary process is
life, being young and hopeful: 'if I had good teeth and my
old job back, then I would enjoy myself.' Her primary
process is the older woman who wants to be younger, but is
growing older instead. She is therefore depressed and
finished with life.

Her primary process claims that she does not want help,
but secondarily there is a younger woman who enjoys life
and says that something should be done to help: to get her
new teeth and a new job. It is this secondary process which
has brought her to the social service station in the first place,
not her primary one which has given up on life and on
trying anything new. The younger woman is still hopeful
while the older one wants to commit suicide.

Frau R. is not asking for membership in the grower's club.
She is not identifying herself as someone interested in help,
but if she really did not want any help at all, she would not
be asking for her teeth and would not be able to constellate a
situation in which others try so hard to help her.

Many older people become depressed because they
identify only with their aging body, the one which cannot
perform as it used to. They turn against life, the inevitability
of existence, those trying to help them and even God. When
Frau R. takes medicine, however, she no longer identifies
with hopelessness.

Frau R.:   Bad thoughts go through my brain. When I take
the medicine, these evil thoughts against God
disappear.

Here she identifies with the one taking the medicine to get rid of her depression. She has flipped and is wanting to feel better, while the evil thoughts against God and life, her nasty moods which we saw before when she said, 'Psychiatric help stinks,' have become secondary in that they are occurring to her. It is dangerous, however, to repress the evil thoughts because this aggression can suddenly turn against her.

The definition developed for psychosis in the section on schizophrenia fits her as well. In a psychosis, the earlier primary process (the young working woman, hopeful about life) flips into a secondary process (the aging phenomenon) so that aging now becomes primary and the old hopeless woman polarizes a new secondary one, the woman who is trying to heal herself and get better. Drugs achieve this process reversal once again so that as long as Frau R. takes them she feels that life is worthwhile. Then the negative thoughts, temporarily repressed, become autonomous, secondary and drop out of awareness.

WORKING WITH THE TOTAL PROCESS
In the midst of a depressed episode, Frau R. is identified with the process of being angry and hopeless about life for not giving her the youthfulness, pleasure and mechanical abilities she once had. Though there are fleeting moments in which she switches and seems to want help, by and large she is against life.

As long as we are unclear about the structure of her process, we are bound to take the unoccupied part in her pattern. In Frau R.'s pattern, the unoccupied part is the healer who is trying to get her to live. In her depressed and nasty state, the more she hears about help, the more she rejects it. The more she rejects it, the more she splits off her secondary request for help and the more the social worker, psychiatrist, psychotherapist, hospitals and police are trapped into trying to be helpful.

This is a vicious and dangerous cycle because if we constantly act like helpers, she never gets the chance to help herself and is constantly in the position of the depressed one who wants to die. But this situation can be reversed by knowing the process structure well enough to flip the two processes.

After trying for about twenty minutes to be the helper and attempting different approaches, I decided to side with the dying process since everything else resulted in negative feedback. Thus I played her primary process better than she could, hoping that she would take on the social worker's process of being helpful and hopeful. I looked down and spoke slowly and in a depressed voice:

Arny: I am now ready to go. Nothing worked, nothing helps. I want to go off alone and think it all over. Nothing can be done here anyway. Too bad.

Frau R.:   No, I am happy that you are here.

I noticed that this was her first positive response and I was genuinely surprised to see that my plan had actually worked.

Arny: Really?

Frau R.:   Yes. For me you are a stranger and it was a great help and a good thing that I could talk about such intimate things with you. I am even getting good at talking about myself [she giggles].

Social Worker: Frau R., that is the first time I have *ever* seen you laugh!

Arny: Give me a coffee, I have had enough here and want to go.

The social worker did not notice what I was doing and said:

Social Worker: Arny, do you not see any chance for helping her? Stay!

Frau R.:   Yes! Do you see any possibility of helping me? Now I would be really interested if you could tell me something helpful!

EVALUATION AND PROGNOSIS

I stayed for a few more minutes and worked with her by putting most of the responsibility for the future in her hands. Remember that a few moments before she had said, 'I hate talking . . . why would you have the feeling you should help me anyhow? I do not expect it.' Now her position has completely reversed and she is saying, 'I am happy that you are here. . . . It was a great help and a good thing that I could talk about such intimate things with you. I am even getting good at talking about myself.'

My taking the position of the depressed and hopeless person helped Frau R. pick up a secondary process, the process of life and being interested in help and therapy. A smile from a chronically and severely depressed person is positive feedback. It should be mentioned, however, that one reason why she became optimistic is because I was congruently fed up with trying to help her. I was not just playing a depressed role. At first, like everyone else around her, I really wanted to help her. Only when I saw that it was a waste of time and energy could I really act as if I was finished helping her.

The fact that she smiled for the first time since she came to the social work station is not yet grounds for optimism. Frau R. would need continued treatment of this kind in a social service network. This means that everyone would have to be informed about the nature of her process and instructed on how to follow it. Since this was a one-time supervision seminar, such instruction was not possible. Under these circumstances, her process of hopelessness was bound to continue. Less than a year later she succeeded in killing herself.

DEPRESSION AS COMPENSATION

In the 1980s, being depressed and hopeless cannot only be seen as a compensation to the Judeo-Christian tradition but to the psychotherapeutic paradigm of helping and healing as well. Not every patient fulfills this paradigm. In fact, trying to be helpful to a patient whose primary process is hopelessness is a dangerous undertaking, based on an inappropriate paradigm and a bad working hypothesis because helpfulness polarizes the secondary process even more, and you create a situation in which the helper must be resisted. Furthermore being helpful to a client who is not primarily interested in help is a goal mismatch and is bound to isolate the client even more than she or he already is.

PSYCHOSIS AND THE METACOMMUNICATOR

The kinds of depressive processes normally seen by the psychiatrist or psychologist in private practice are depressions with a metacommunicator. Someone within the client is coming for help, somebody is present who is not depressed but is concerned about the depression and wants a cure for it.

This is not the case with Frau R. She is not coming to the social service center primarily for psychiatric help, but because she wants a new set of teeth. According to her statements, she has already had enough psychiatric help. Hence, there is no one present to discuss the seriousness of her depression. There are only a few choices available in such a case. You can help her by giving her psychopharmica, assuming that the metacommunicator is strong enough to want to take these pills. You can try to be helpful and begin to hate her because she resists help, you can send her to somebody else instead of challenging yourself or you can try, and probably fail, at giving her insight into her depression. The only other possibility I know of is to study her process structure and enter it with awareness.

THE PURPOSE OF DEPRESSION

Instead of treating depression as if it were something we should overcome, we can also ask what its meaning is. For example, what was the usefulness in my giving up and going home to think it over? From the material at hand, we can see that if a depressed and hopeless experience is allowed to come up, then the road is cleared for help.

Instead of constantly resisting the processes in front of us, we might stop and admit to their presence. Instead of hoping that the world will be saved by the scientists, theologians and politicians, I wonder what would happen if everyone in a given community would face all of the depressing and disturbing facts in our lives and risk being depressed by them. Only by risking a depression in this way is a road for possible creative solutions to the future prepared for.

OCCUPATION THEORY

When faced with an impasse in our world, most of us become optimists and try to find the solution to the impasse, imagining we have found it even when we have not. Such a world needs Frau R. and others who become depressed to sober up false and unbased optimism. If we understand the world as a round table, then there is going to have to be at least one chair for a depressed person if the other three are filled with optimists. The depressed one sees that the world is coming to an end, but, unlike the optimist, is unconvinced by the imagined solutions. The existential hopelessness of the depressed person is the bottom line, the beginning of facing the facts and of constellating new and creative solutions to life.

Intrapsychically, we can imagine a field or round table in Frau R: three people are depressed and are balanced by a therapist who is trying to help. If the therapist leaves his chair, Frau R. will have to take the one of the optimist. According to occupation theory, every system has to be balanced, whole and complete, just as an atom with an extra valence searches to combine with another atom and so attain balance.

HOLOGRAM THEORY

The inner personal situation reflects the outer one and vice versa. We see with Frau R. that the outer world carries the same pattern as the inner one. This speculation is a form of hologram theory since a hologram is a piece of material, like glass, which carries a particular pattern. If the glass breaks, then each of the parts of the glass carry the same pattern as the whole.

Seeing the world through the analogy of hologram theory helps you understand how you can change the individual by working with the world or change the world by working with the individual. Thus there are two ways of working with hopeless situations, extreme states and impossible clients. One is by improving the psychotherapy of the individual and the other is by working on the world situation. In this present case, this means understanding the value in looking soberly at a difficult situation. If everyone in Frau R.'s world looked at the state of the planet at the end of the 1980s and considered the apparently catastrophic ecological, social and political problems, a sobering depression might be followed with new and creative solutions not presently part of our naïve hope and belief in human know-how. What would happen to the world is uncertain, but it is likely that Frau R. and others like her would want to help those who are hopeless.

The meaning of Frau R. for the world can be applied to psychology as well. It seems to me that psychology is too optimistic. Most psychologists and psychiatrists are naïvely hopeful and radiate good will even when they do not know what they are doing. For example, the entire area of psychotic states is still in a pioneering period. The discovery of the simplest structures to these 'disorders' is at a stage which is equivalent to that of physics at the time Galileo discovered that gravity exerts an accelerating force.

We are just learning about the forces and effects which move people and we need to be very humble and respectful of processes which we barely understand and get these processes and the people who manifest them to show us the way. Frau R. is just right for the present state of psychology because she powerfully reminds us of the fact that the course of nature is not in the hands of the therapist.

Chapter 9
THE MANIC SAVIOR

Frau P. was invited to the social service station this morning because the program director thought it might be a good opportunity for the city authorities, with whom she was previously in conflict, to see her now in a calm and 'normal' state of mind. It seems Frau P., during a manic episode, took it upon herself to help her entire village. On any one day she was in contact with dozens of townspeople and city authorities, and disturbed her immediate environment to such a degree that she was finally interned in a mental hospital. Now she is about to return to ordinary life after her stay in the hospital.

Everyone is present this morning: Frau P., the local staff, two other social workers from the area, the chief of the social services for this district of Switzerland, a city authority whom Frau P. had previously bothered, Joe and I.

Frau P. sits in her chair wearing a colorful skirt. Her right hand is holding her left elbow, her left hand is supporting her head in a position I have frequently seen among people who are sad, depressed and trying to support themselves. In working with such a posture, it frequently turns out that the hand holding the head is a supporting figure such as the mother. The head which is being supported is the child. It is not difficult to guess Frau P.'s primary and secondary process from her first few sentences and her body posture.

Frau P.: I do not want to speak about myself but of other
people's problems. I heard of others who had

problems and tried to get to the bottom of them. I
made a lot of contact with these people. I tried to
find their private problems. There were a great deal
of misunderstandings which they suffered from. It
was difficult to find solutions. One woman with-
drew from the world because her neighbor was not
friendly with her. It is difficult to say . . . she
needed help with her environment, help in her
household. I have found much injustice, especially
where people needed a 'middle-man,' a helper . . .
but I have also learned that one cannot just go
forward and try to make solutions. It does not help.

PROCESS STRUCTURE

In the first place, we notice that she has a metacommunicator. At the moment she is neither in an extreme state nor
psychotic. Her primary process adapts to the world around
her; she sounds psychologically insightful.

She identifies herself as not being interested in her own
problems, but in those of others. She is a helper, someone
who helps troubled people and someone who realizes that
she cannot force solutions. Since she is strongly interested in
the misunderstandings and conflicts of others in her primary
process, she is like a social worker or even a family
therapist.

The secondary process consists of the figures 'myself'
whom she does not want to talk about and also 'the people
who have private problems' and suffer from misunderstandings and injustice. We can summarize her secondary process
as people who need help with the environment.

WORKING WITH FRAU P.

How do you work with a person who does not want to work
on him or herself? One way is to take her primary process at
its face value and just listen to her stories about others. But
since this is what happens to her in everyday life, it won't
be the most satisfying solution.

Another possibility is to think that the people she talks
about are parts of herself and thus she will eventually turn

towards herself and ask for help. The weakness with this method is that it does not respect her wish not to talk about herself. Though it is a normal therapeutic intervention, it is no match for her primary process and is thus bound to get negative feedback.

A third possible intervention is to ignore what she says altogether and practice your own methods of intervention with her. Ask her for dreams, get her to act out the other people or press her about her feelings. If I worked privately with her I might be tempted to work with her hand and arm signals which I mentioned above. Yet I am sure my own interests would get me nowhere and that I would be forced to try the following method: taking her interest in others seriously and asking her to learn how to really help them. This means learning how to get along with others, obtaining some sort of social or psychological education or perhaps even learning how to confront people. She needs a teacher who will press her to report accurately on what she does with people and what kind of feedback it gets.

In this way she would simultaneously learn the tools of psychology and discover how to work with herself. No doubt this is the way most psychologists learn to work with themselves. A lot of their interest in others is connected to projections of their own problems. Through learning to work with others, their own problems are indirectly worked on.

There is a belief, however, among different schools of psychotherapy that one should first work on oneself and then help others. This is a belief unique to the grower's club, and at the moment I am not yet sure that Frau P. belongs to this club. I noticed that as soon as she said she did not want to talk about herself, everyone in the circle, the analysts, social workers and city officials, got very upset. They do not agree that she should do what she wants, namely, try and help others. The following response is from the city official whom she irritated during the acute phase of her most recent episode.

City official: I am impressed with you today Frau P. I
               notice that you can now listen to us. Don't think that

what I said about you earlier, in your previous
condition, was so negative that one would think that
you were crazy. Now you are quiet and no longer
aggressive. Now you are peaceful, positive and
stabilized. In the past you did not sleep or eat!

Frau P. first looks down at her watch, then quickly at the
rug and then looks up and says quietly:

Frau P.: But for me it was not bad to eat only a little for
several days. And I did not miss sleeping.
City official (placatingly, as if to a child): But you called us
constantly and bothered us incessantly.
Frau P. (directly, almost angrily): Only when it was urgent.

CONVERSATION PROCESS
The authority acts, in his primary process, as if he were a
good man who cared for others. Secondarily, he double
signals to her that she is crazy by saying: 'Don't think that
what I said about you earlier . . . was so negative that one
would think that you were crazy.' Frau P. feels misunderstood
by him, just like the people she talked about. But feeling
misunderstood and needing help is a secondary process,
primarily she is carrying on a nice social conversation like
everyone else. Nevertheless she is irritated by the insinu-
ation that she is a crazy, sick and aggressive woman. The
message she experiences is, 'Cool off baby or you'll go back
to the nut house!'
   The problem with the conversation is not that the city
official thinks that she is nuts but that he and she are both
unable to express themselves directly. He too needs to learn
about communication so he could express his messages
directly and not have to double signal them. I am certain
that if he could, he would have said to her at the times she
bothered him, 'Listen lady, cool off or I am going to call the
authorities and have you interned. You better believe me,
you bug me too much!'
   Certainly this would have been difficult for him to do, for
no one wants to be nasty. On the other hand, by not being

direct and only double signalling his irritation to her, the mental institutions were left to pick her up and calm her down with drugs.

Moreover, the city official's difficulty in standing for what he thinks is similar to Frau P.'s problem. She, too, feels guilty about what she thinks, namely that the official misunderstands her. Not eating during her episode was not a serious problem for her and she had trouble asserting this directly to the official.

Though I tried to take the focus off her and put it on the entire interaction, Frau P. and I were alone in this intention. Near the end of the conversation, after I had tried to focus on the group interaction while the others tried to change her, she said:

Frau P.: I am not content because all our talk centered around me.

A therapist: But we wanted to learn how to get along with you better, that is the problem.

City official: For me this has been a very positive experience, I liked it. It gave me a chance to see you again, to meet you when you are not on medicine.

Frau P.: I know that I made a lot of problems, it is not so funny. [She laughs.]

LAUGHTER

Why does she laugh? The situation is really amusing. There are three different goals and viewpoints. Frau P. is interested in others. The official is interested in cooling her down and the therapist is interested in working with her. But there is even a fourth viewpoint, mine. I was interested in the entire interaction scene! What else can you do but laugh? We might easily have been talking English, German, French and Italian!

The scene vaguely reminds me of Ken Kesey's novel, *One Flew Over the Cuckoo's Nest*. The book deals with the attempt to repress a madly creative and wonderful guy who was disturbing the environment. The psychiatrists and nurses gave him electroshock treatment to cool him off and make him normal. A greater perspective on the city or group problem was obviously missing in that fictional story and, as you can see for yourself, here as well. The officials and therapists want to cool off Frau P.'s manic behavior while she is only interested in the betterment of mankind.

CHANGE

Who should change? If Frau P. could concentrate on her own problems she would calm down the environment. If the official would study his own interaction difficulties he would realize that he, too, is unconscious and needs to change. When the therapist wakes up, he will change his attitude and stop concentrating solely on Frau P.

I can only guess about Frau P.'s possible changes because we did not work therapeutically with her. One of her personal problems did come out in the midst of the interview which indicates how and where she needs help. Her ex-husband took her children from her custody and she could not defend herself properly. She did her best, however, by throwing an hysterical fit as the kids were taken away. She suffered immensely, but could not sufficiently support herself. Thus she swallowed the whole problem and became a manic helper for other women in the city who had been misunderstood.

THE COLLECTIVE'S CHANGE

In Switzerland, as in other countries, custody of the children usually goes to the mother. This is due to many factors, among them the fact that women are not used to defending themselves in public against city officials. Thus, the laws compensate for this by favoring their interests.

Women's liberation has also tried to increase the support given to women, but laws and liberation movements are not enough. Women and men alike need training in communication so that everyone can work together better. Since women frequently suffer from their inability to defend themselves in the community, Frau P. must play the Joan of Arc role for those who are being victimized. Frau P. thus compensates the way most of us behave in the community.

Few women or men stand up and turn the county courthouse upside down in an effort to find out which women have not been cared for sufficiently.

We need a broader perspective in psychiatry and social work. We need to look at the entire communication network and work with Frau P. as well as the world she is living in, the world which she compensates and teaches. Focusing *only* upon Frau P.'s problems would mean ignoring the cultural problems she is compensating. People not only need more protection from the city authorities but encouragement in developing the necessary personal strength to stand up in public and defend their individual viewpoints. Relying on the police, lawyers, psychologists and city government officials is a way of ignoring our own development and worldly responsibilities.

The story of Frau P. thus shows us again that the individual is disturbed by and suffers from the city, while the city suffers from the commotion made by the individual in an extreme state. Once again we see that solving the problems of an individual who suffers from extreme states is inextricably intertwined with the city's problems.

Part IV
DRUG ABUSE

Chapter 10
HEROIN

According to the World Health Organization, drug addiction is the need to increase the dosage of a drug which is destructive to the individual and environment in order to maintain or increase its effect. Common addictive drugs are alcohol, heroin, morphium, methadone, cocaine, amphetamines and related compounds.

This definition of addiction leaves undefined the nature of the drug and its destructive effects. For example, there are physiological and psychological addictions to cigarette smoking, coffee and black tea. Behavior associated with taking these drugs may actually meet the above definition for addiction: occasional overactivity which is disturbing to the environment. In the case of marijuana or hashish, the addiction may have minimal physical consequences for the user, but could place him in the position of community scapegoat.

ENDORPHINES
Studies of addiction and drugs are complicated by the fact that the body itself is capable of producing mind and mood altering drugs called 'endorphines.' This term is derived from 'endogenous morphine.' Endorphines refer to any naturally occurring substance in the brain or tissue having pharmacological effects resembling opiate alkaloids such as morphine or heroin.

Opiate-like effects from the body's own endorphine production occur during such ordinary activities as long-distance running, meditation, yoga or other calming and relaxing sports. Are these activities addictive? They can also be dangerous for the individual and may also be associated with conflicts and disturbances in the environment.

COLLECTIVE ATTITUDES TOWARDS DRUGS

Western interest in drugs dates back to the beginning of written history, though recent interest in heroin and its derivatives has flourished because of its increased use among young people. Collective opinion about drugs is widely divergent. Mind researchers like Andrew Weil (1972) have promoted the use of drugs as an aid to exploring altered states of consciousness while the general public views drugs as ruinous to one's health and well being.

Drug research has shown that the extent of organic brain intoxication depends upon the individual's psychology. By analogy the effects of brain damage upon the individual also depend upon the psychology of the person affected. My experience with many drug takers verifies Weil's idea that drugs do not cause altered states, but open doors to these states. Whether or not the drug user goes through the door depends upon his individual situation. Thus many shamans use drugs to assist them in their spiritual adventures. For example, don Juan, Castaneda's mentor, uses them to help his students, but claims that they are unnecessary.

Collective opinion about drugs stems from the fear of altered states which is perceived as a threat to everyday reality (cf. Weil, 1972). The social conflicts, neurophysiological considerations and spiritual states connected with drugs are issues of great interest to those in the mental health profession, especially since medicine is now the main user of mind altering drugs! The question remains as to who chooses to use these mind altering drugs and when the choice is to be made. However, I want to keep to my main topic, and refer the interested reader to the literature.

WORKING WITH HERR C.

Let us keep these general remarks about drugs in mind as we listen to Herr C., a long-time heroin addict who has become dependent upon the city's hospitals, drug clinics and social welfare agencies for medical, moral and financial aid. Herr C., twenty-eight years old, suffers from the many typical problems connected with heroin addiction.

John, one of the social workers, is sitting in a chair talking to Herr C. as I walk in. John informs me that Herr C. has been addicted to heroin for more than nine years. He goes through periodic cycles of addiction and withdrawal. With the help of medication, he appears to be 'cured,' but then falls back onto heroin for one of many reasons. John seems to be aiming his therapeutic endeavors at discovering the feelings and reasons behind Herr C.'s addiction.

Herr C. begins to describe to us some of the details of his heroin problem. He is sitting in a relaxed position and speaks with a slight slur, most likely due to the consumption of sleeping pills which are meant to aid the withdrawal from methadone, which is itself used to ease the withdrawal from heroin. He speaks in a rapid although slurred tempo which does not allow much chance for us to respond.

Herr C.: Heroin attacks the central nervous system, right? Feelings are more intense on heroin. The longer you are on the poison the more you like to shoot it. I can't say what it's all about, but it's wild. After shooting it up, what comes later is absolute contentment.

I get aggressive when I am on heroin. Of course I am also aggressive when I am withdrawing. Once, while I was kicking the habit, someone at the hospital where I was said to me that I should help wash the dishes. I picked up the dish rag and threw it at him. He should have left me in peace. I had so much going on with myself that I didn't want to have to relate to anyone.

PROCESS STRUCTURE
Herr C.'s primary process, that which he identifies with, is all aspects of taking heroin. He shoots it up, he gets aggressive while taking it, he picks up objects and throws

them while withdrawing and he gets angry if he is not left in peace. While withdrawing, he is so busy with himself that he has no interest in relating. I notice this lack of interest with us in his tempo: he talks so quickly that no one else but he can speak.

His primary process is similar to that of many addicts. He actually identifies with heroin itself. 'Heroin attacks the central nervous system,' and, since 'The longer you are on the poison, the more you like to shoot it,' we can say that Herr C. himself is a 'poison' which attacks the central nervous system or anything that might give him the impulse to work and disturb his peace.

Thus, like the old adage which states that 'you are what you eat,' Herr C. is heroin. People who are addicted to coffee actually begin to produce coffee-like effects on those around them, just like alcoholics, as we shall see in the next chapter, produce alcoholic effects in their environment.

Herr C.'s secondary process, that which he does not identify with, is portrayed by the man in his story who told him to wash the dishes. 'Cleaning up' and pitching in to the work in his environment is a secondary process with which he is in conflict. It is no coincidence that a slang expression among addicts for getting off heroin is 'cleaning up.'

WORKING WITH HERR C.

It is important to notice that when I describe Herr C.'s psychology I assume that what he says about the states he experiences on heroin are accurate descriptions of what he feels now. The reason for this assumption is that if you are able to verbally formulate something, it is true in that moment.

His total process includes a metacommunicator. He is able to talk about his states in contrast to drugged states in which the chemistry of the body is so altered that a metacommunicator appears to be absent. His process can be described as a conflict between heroin, the tyrannical protector of peacefulness, and the collective interests of 'cleaning up' and working. The entire process behaves in a holographic fashion which Herr C. carries into his environment. Whenever he is the one most interested in peace, he will have conflicts with others interested in keeping the world in order. Now he is bound to have a conflict with us.

Herr C.:   I dropped the recent withdrawal attempt at the hospital because it was too tough for me. Do you understand, John?

John nods his head.

Arny (to Herr C.):   Apparently John understands but what I don't understand is why you won't promise John, as he has required many times in this conversation already, to call him when you have problems instead of just taking heroin and giving up on your attempted withdrawal.

John: Yes, please Herr C., do come and call me when you need me.

Arny   (escalating the conflict):   There you are, trying to weasel out of getting off heroin again. I want you to promise that you will call!

While reviewing the tape, I notice that at this point Herr C. shakes his head very gently from side to side, indicating 'no' but says:

Herr C.:   I would like to call . . . I promise . . . right?

I did not see his double signal implying 'no' while talking to him. Therefore I unconsciously doubted his promise.

Arny: Is it possible that you are really promising to call?

John: If you would come and talk, it would be better for you, Herr C.

Herr C.:   Yes, but you know as soon as I get out of the hospital, heroin is around. It is on the tram, in the street, in front of my door. It is so easy to get and take when I do not call you.

I raise my voice again and try to escalate the conflict:

Arny: There you are again, trying to weasel out. You first
intend to withdraw and then find an excuse to get
addicted again. So I don't believe that you want to
withdraw.

Herr C.: You have to understand that when you're on
heroin you don't think. Do you understand?

Arny: You are lazy and weasling out of thinking!

The tenseness of the struggle upsets John and he changes
the subject:

John: But what do you feel when you withdraw?

THE WITHDRAWAL ISSUE

Herr C. is trying to explain his difficult situation to John and
me but we do not understand that withdrawing is difficult,
that he gets too tired to call for help, that heroin is
everywhere, that thinking is difficult when on heroin and,
finally, that he wants peace and does not want to 'clean up.'

After reviewing the tapes, I think Herr C. is correct to say
that I did not understand him. He has helped me change the
way I work with heroin addicts. I understand now that
getting off heroin is difficult because what it is like to be on
heroin is not sufficiently defined and understood.

You cannot work with a state unless you know what it is.
For example, as we saw in the previous chapters, you
cannot work well with schizophrenia if you use cultural
definitions to understand it. So let us see exactly what state
Herr C. is talking about and see how we could have used
his descriptions of the heroin or withdrawing states in order
to work with him.

He complains that he is tired and cannot call for help
when he needs it because heroin is easier to get than
psychotherapy. The discussion proceeds as if we are talking
about a process in the past and not one which is also going
on right NOW. Right now Herr C. is exhausted. Right now
he is not calling and not asking for help. Right now, with

us, all he wants is money from the agency, methadone to ease his pain and sleeping pills to make him sleepier.

For Herr C., heroin is a state which inhibits thinking and promotes peace. At the moment with us he does not want to think, he wants peace from life, from trouble, from thinking, from working and from us. And the way he deals with us is the way he deals with all of his conflicts: he filters out his own anger towards the world which wants him to work and agrees to change, while feeling that he won't. Knowing this structure, we could either take up his secondary process of cleaning up and fight with his lazy primary process, or we could take over the primary process by relaxing and going against consensus reality as he does. The approach which gets the best feedback depends upon the client and therapist.

ENVIRONMENTAL SUPPORT FOR ADDICTION
Herr C.'s present environment supports heroin addiction and the tendency to avoid difficulties. We saw above how the social worker had trouble with the escalating tension between Herr C. and me when I pressed him to admit that he did not want to withdraw. In order to avoid the tension and ensuing conflict, John asked him about his feelings.

As part of the environment, John creates a 'heroin-like' process by asking about feelings and trying to avoid the conflict. In this way, the therapist makes heroin available by postponing the pain of withdrawal. Talking about heroin as if it existed only in the past or probable future is a way of avoiding Herr C.'s current state of not wanting, or not being able, to think and work.

WORKING WITH THE HEROIN STATE
Thus I work with such a discussion today by pointing out to the individual that he is now on heroin, every time he refuses to think, every time he refuses to meet a conflict, even every time he slouches. I would point out to him how he is on heroin *now* whether or not he has taken it. Intoxication is a state which occurs with or without the real drug. The real drug makes the state more available to the

individual, but the state is there before the drug!

Upon knowing this, each client will react differently and what I do depends upon which process is in the foreground. One type of addict is shocked to realize that she *now* behaves as if on heroin and reacts by immediately producing a sober state. Other addicts will begin to analyze why they want to leave their feelings and why they do not want to be here. Like those who have experienced extreme states without drugs, they complain how depressing the world is. These people need help in learning how to deal with painful problems and how to reduce their pain.

Another kind of addict might refuse to admit that he is in a heroin state. In this case, I would ask him to act as if he were on heroin, to feel, move and appear the way he would when on it. He would then realize that heroin is a state independent of the real drug. With others who refuse to consciously access the heroin state or who are too drugged to even talk, I myself could act as if I were drugged and ask them for help. This type of intervention operates in the same way as in psychotic states. A process reversal occurs and the addict takes over the role of the psychologist trying to help me clean up. The potential for this reversal frequently makes addicts excellent therapists in drug clinics after kicking their habit.

Still there is another group of drug takers who are really hidden shamans and who need help in investigating the far reaches of their own human potential. These people often turn out to be psychic researchers of the future, wanting and needing tools to enter, deal with and investigate the entire human condition. They need to learn the ins and outs of working with altered states, processing their own material and learning methods and procedures of body work and psychology.

ON THE USE OF THE PAST

Talking about heroin as if it were a problem of the past or a potential future problem is not very helpful for the addict. One of the functions of telling stories as if they were in the past or future is to convince the story teller and the listener that the events are unalterable. The future and past tenses have an hypnotic effect on the listener and teller. For example, Herr C. states that when he left the hospital, heroin was readily available. One thinks that this is an unalterable situation. Whether or not the situation can be changed is a subject for debate. Pointing out how heroin is readily available now makes the addict's present state more accessible to alteration.

Descriptions of the future and the past are not only accompanied by the implication that they cannot be altered but also by hopelessness. Talking of the past and future hypnotizes us into believing that nothing can be changed, the world is the way it is, everything is just a game anyhow and life is worthless.

CULTURAL REACTIONS

These messages are carried by many young people today and provoke the establishment to be against drugs. The young person on drugs who is supposed to be going out and conquering life is, in the minds of his elders, giving up because he is depressed, hopeless, or angry at the social structure around him. Therefore simply revolting against the junkie by trying to wipe out heroin addiction will not solve the tension and differences of belief between the old and the young.

Mao's solution to the drug problem was to force withdrawal by detainment in a work camp. Clearly Mao is going to have a greater cure rate than any western drug clinic, which at best claims that 30 percent of the addicts successfully withdraw. Though successful, such pressure does not take into consideration the counter-culture aspects of drug taking, the fact that part of the addict's message is that the world as it is is unacceptable.

HERR C.'s FUTURE

In the interview with Herr C. the process which is likely to happen to him is already implicit in what he says.

Herr C.:   If I do not make it this time in withdrawing, then you can forget me. You can give me methadone

until the end of my life, until I die. You can forget
me. Terribly simple. That is that. Finished.

Today, I would deal with this statement by amplifying its
tough and militaristic tone. I would say to Herr C., 'Well, I
feel badly that you may die, but I like the way you cleaned
up your thinking and can now be concise. I notice how you
speak about yourself without sentiment and regret and
therefore I will not give you methadone any longer than two
weeks. If you can make it off heroin by then, fine. If not, I
shall, as you advise me to, forget you. As you say, it's
terribly simple. That is that. Finished. Come back in two
weeks and we'll see what to do next. I like your brevity!'

Chapter 11
ALCOHOL

Before hearing about Herr G., let us discuss the facts about alcohol. At least 20 percent of the western world is either directly addicted to alcohol or else connected to the alcoholic through family ties. Some texts say that 50 percent of all arrests in the United States and in Europe are associated with alcohol consumption (Freedman, 1980, p. 676). Alcoholism is a widespread problem. The public views the alcoholic as a disturbed and problematical social disgrace, though alcohol is simultaneously the most socially acceptable mind altering drug available. Though alcoholism has been a public difficulty since ancient times, there is, in my opinion, very little known about how it operates. To demonstrate this I would like to recommend that the reader takes part in the following experiment.

EXPERIMENTING WITH ALCOHOL
Do you remember the last time you drank a large quantity of beer or wine? Were you alone or at a party? Can you recall the atmosphere? Can you remember why you drank? This is undoubtedly a difficult question. What were your reasons? Were you uncomfortable with some problem or some person, were you depressed or nervous? Did you want to get over your inhibitions, or did you want to forget an outer problem or a part of yourself?

Now try to reaccess the drunken state. Try to act drunk: move, think, feel, see, talk and relate to others as if you were inebriated. Now, in your present drunken state,

121

answer the following questions. How has your ability to relate to others changed? Do you feel pain when you pinch yourself in the arm or in the cheek? Do you recall painful memories? What is in the foreground of your awareness?

ALCOHOL: FACT OR FICTION?

Through this experiment I hope you discover that being drunk, stoned or 'high' does not depend upon alcohol or heroin. You can access a drunken state without drinking anything. If you compare the answers you get in the state that you just accessed to the answers you get when you really drink something, you will be surprised to discover that they are quite similar.

The ability to access a state is a power we all have. We can alter our states of consciousness at will as well as with the help of drugs, dreams, hypnotism and psychosis. This ability of ours is what causes the placebo effect and other mind over matter phenomena. The very suggestion that our pain will diminish prompts us to access a less painful state, regardless of whether we take real aspirin or a placebo. Naturally, this can also happen in the reverse.

INTRODUCING HERR G.

By this time I hope you have realized that being an alcoholic means having a preference for a certain state of consciousness. Let's use a beginner's mind to work with this state. Let us access this beginner's mind now as we meet Herr G.

Herr G. stumbles into the social service station at around 9.30 am after having a breakfast of some thirty beers. He sits down and waits politely for the interview to begin. He moves forwards and looks down at the floor. He seems unhappy, but then looks up suddenly when he is spoken to as if he were embarrassed about being caught in his thoughts.

He is a heavy-set man in his middle fifties and looks drunk: he switches his sitting position unexpectedly, wipes his head awkwardly and uncoordinatedly, and points a wobbly finger while he talks, a finger that sometimes aims at the person he is talking to and sometimes does not. There is a time lag between what he says and the body gestures he uses in association with his words. His laughter is abrupt and a bit rough, unrelated to what he or others say. He will ask the same thing three or four times, as if he were not listening or could not remember the answer. We have the impression that he is not quite here.

Sitting with Herr G. this morning are Joe, Ron, who is Herr G.'s therapist, Sally and myself. The content of the conversation will soon reveal a tragic accident which, however unfortunate, seems to happen often in alcoholic couples. Several weeks ago, Herr G.'s wife, who was also an alcoholic, in the midst of a binge stumbled and fell into their dog's straw basket. A piece of straw went through her throat and killed her.

Herr G. still has a lot of feeling wrapped up with this tragedy. His main issue turns out to be the guilt associated with her death and the question of having the courage to clean up his own problems. The interview begins as follows.

Ron: I would like to introduce Arny and Joe to you, Herr G. They are here this week to supervise our work.
Herr G (looking confused): Arny?
Ron: Arny.
Herr G: Arny?
Ron: Arny.
Herr G. (thoughtfully): Arny.
Ron: Yes, Arny.

From this interaction, one could surmise that Herr G. is drunk, has an organic brain syndrome, has short-term memory loss or is not occupying his ability to hear. But the question is, why? What is the function of not being able to remember a name and of acting drunk? Is he trying to forget something? Is he listening to something else internally? We could have worked with this by saying, 'Don't listen to us, listen to yourself.' The conversation, however, went differently.

Ron: How are you? What have you been doing?
Herr G. (laughing):   You know Ron, . . . I like you. You always ask such stupid questions.

Ron ignores this negative feedback and perseveres.

Ron: What did you do yesterday?
Herr G.:   I called my mother.
Ron: Why didn't you go directly and talk to her?
Herr G.:   I had a nice talk with her on the phone.
Ron: Was she upset that you didn't go to see her?

Herr G. responds slowly, apparently irritated, but nevertheless with a smile

Herr G.:   Again, those stupid questions . . . I did not have the courage to . . .

I wait a while for him to continue. Then I say:

Arny: You did not have the courage to do what?
Herr G. [pause]:   It takes a lot of courage to say . . . I am . . . I am . . . like I am . . . a fool.

PROCESS STRUCTURE

Herr G. has a metacommunicator. Despite his drunken state, he takes great pride in discussing his states and making judgements upon himself. Hence we could, if we wanted to, even ask him to change states. What are his states? Herr G.'s primary process is to act drunk and be the fool, a weakling who does not have the courage to admit it. He lacks courage. He is very good at making people feel well around him by smiling at us, but in fact he does not stand for what he thinks. He did not like Ron's questions, but did not tell him to stop. Instead, he ignored the question about his mother and changed the subject.

His secondary process is having the courage to criticize himself and others. He said to Ron, 'You . . . ask . . . stupid questions.' He says it with a laugh, however, and does not identify with this 'courageous' part of himself.

This is the information about the process structure available to us one minute and twenty seconds after the interview begins. We can now begin to work with it. An interesting idea would be to bring up the secondary process of courage and make it available to him. But before working with someone, it is important to establish a feeling of relationship with them. This means relating to their primary process. In the case of Herr G., a relationship means, to begin with at least, not only feeling my way into his life situation, but also, by means of noting his signals and pacing the tempo of his talk, relating to him as one drunk to another.

Arny (laughing, speaking slowly and gesturing in Herr G.'s tempo):   Oh, you know . . . I am a fool too, yeah. . . .

Joe (picking up the atmosphere):   Me too, I have failed many times.

Herr G.:   Really, you too?

Another social worker joins in and says:

Social worker: I have failed too, twenty-six times.

Herr G.:   If I am honest . . . then . . . I have to admit . . . that I have failed . . . only once.

Arny: Not me, I fail once every five minutes.

Herr G.:   You guys are a gift to me.

Everyone laughs and the atmosphere becomes very warm and friendly. I want to stress, however, that while we have been successful in feeling our way into Herr G.'s process, there is a danger that by pacing and mirroring the client, we enter into the same state. Hence, we could begin to relax in the warm atmosphere and lose our relativity. The alcoholic state here is one of warmth and brotherly love. It is so powerful that it can put a whole room in a similar state. In this way, the alcoholic is alcohol: he is like a drink for us, and if we want to work with him we have to be careful not to drink too much.

Ron aims at bringing up the content which was previously missing in the conversation, assuming that Herr G. was avoiding the problematical topic of his wife's death.

Ron: What have you failed at exactly?

Herr G.:   Now pick this up with your camera. Pick this up Arny. I need the courage to say that in life, to say . . . to say . . . [pointing to Ron] to say . . . that I have failed once in my life. Ron, we have fought with one another. . . . We . . . if I have to be honest . . . [crying] . . . we talked . . . Ron . . . what is life? What is life? [Pointing again at Ron, now vehemently.] What is life? (Now to me.) Arny what is life?

Arny: Herr G., what is life?

Herr G.:   Life is shitty. . . . Did someone say I was sad . . . I am . . . sad . . . [now slowly, quietly] . . . about the death of my wife.

He cries, looks down, and covers his eyes. Then suddenly another social worker comes in the room and he raises his head, smiles and greets her.

Herr G.:   Hello, how are you?

MORE ABOUT SECONDARY PROCESSES

His sadness is a secondary process; 'someone' says he is sad. His primary process is to be sociable and nice, to the newcomer in the room, for example. When the social worker enters, he immediately pushes away his sadness.

In addition, Herr G. said that in the past he had fought with Ron. Fighting is a secondary process he cannot stand up for in the present. He only half-heartedly resists Ron. This is in no way an unusual case, however. Most of us are shy about being direct and confronting others. Many of us split off these feelings and therefore experience ourselves as being unrecognized by others. This is the case with Herr G.

Herr G.: I know the reason for her death. She ruined herself slowly. Knowing this makes me unhappy . . . and [pointing his finger at Ron] . . . Ron . . . you are guilty for her death . . . why did she do it . . . why? You are guilty . . . she did not know what do . . . she loved me a lot . . . [breaks down again].

Ron (soothingly and philosophically):   Herr G., sadness is a noble feeling, but you do not understand things properly. You did not cause your wife's death.

Herr G (angrily): Ron, you cannot take my sadness from me!

Herr G. is correct in thinking that Ron is taking his feeling away and replacing it with understanding. But then Ron is not the only one guilty of this, for Herr G. himself dropped his feelings just a moment before when the social worker came in. Herr G. has an internal program called alcohol which invites him and others to drop the feelings they have.

Herr G.: You cannot take my sadness from me . . . but what's the difference. She needed me and she died.

Herr G. cries now, covering his face with both hands. I put my hand on his knee in a gesture of sympathy, waiting while he cries. He puts his hand over mine and then suddenly picks up my hand and moves it away.

Arny: What feeling is being taken from you, Herr G.?
Herr G.: Feeling . . . feeling becomes weak and shallow . . . I am only a human being . . .

THE THERAPIST AS THE DRUG
Just as the therapist can become heroin by helping a client avoid painful tension, so too can he become alcohol by helping a client make feelings weaker and more shallow by sympathy and understanding. Most of us, therapists and

non-therapists alike, are afraid of working with intense emotions. Hence, we tend to cut them off before they have been processed. The result is that the secondary processes of the client cycle and appear only in the form of dreams, fantasies and psychosomatic complaints.

WHO IS THE WIFE?

The death of Herr G.'s wife is a tragic and depressing episode which happened in the past and which Herr G. is now mourning. Nevertheless, I must ask myself who this wife is in Herr G.'s psychology and where she is in his signals. Who is the alcoholic who slowly ruined her life through drinking and who finally and unconsciously committed suicide? Mentioning third parties who are not present is an indication that the figure is present somewhere at that moment.

When consumed over a long period of time, alcohol slowly undermines one's health by disturbing the liver, the nervous system and the pancreas. Hence, the wife represents that part of Herr G.'s present personality which is in the midst of unconsciously committing suicide. If he continues to drink as heavily as he does now, he will injure his physical health either through the effect of alcohol or through an accident. She is his own hidden potential for accidental suicide.

THE THERAPIST'S GUILT

Herr G. is right to be angry at Ron. I have no idea whether Ron was guilty of letting Herr G.'s wife die. But the present danger is that Ron is not forceful enough with Herr G., who himself is in danger of dying.

It is useful to amplify a client's criticism. In this case, the therapist will eventually have to admit that he has not only failed with the wife but is failing with Herr G. too. Ron is not succeeding with Herr G.'s alcoholism. It could possibly be useful for Ron to admit that he is not only failing now, but may fail altogether in clearing up Herr G.'s addiction! An addiction which has successfully possessed someone for thirty years, which almost seems to be inherited, as it does in some cases, and which determines so much of the client's life may, in fact, never be 'curable.' A therapist who admits his weakness in the face of such a problem is not just being honest but is also asking the client for help. Two people working with a demon may do better than one or none at all.

FLIPPING WITH THE CLIENT'S HOLOGRAM

The occupation phenomenon in which all parts of a pattern must be occupied can cause a serious problem for a therapist. In Herr G.'s situation, for example, when he is the weak one who avoids difficult feelings, Ron becomes the courageous one trying to get to the truth. Then, when Herr G. begins to tell his true feelings, the occupation of the pattern flip-flops and Ron reframes Herr G.'s sadness, trying to avoid the feelings.

The same structure organizes all the other interactions around an alcoholic. When one member of a couple drinks, he deadens certain perceptions, like alcohol itself. In order to live with him, however, the other member must also deaden those perceptions. He is alcohol, and she drinks it and her perceptions die. She in turn becomes like alcohol for him, a perception deadener. We have two people in one process consisting of a drinker and the drink being drunk. The situation flips when the partner of the alcoholic gets angry at the alcoholic, makes a nasty threat, but, like a weakling, never carries the threat to completion. During this phase of the relationship the alcoholic gets very tough and reacts violently. The flip-flop process could be useful, but it usually occurs unconsciously and is therefore hurtful, dangerous and tragic.

This process structure can be used at any time with anyone in an altered state. When an alcoholic acts drunk, a schizophrenic mad, a heroin addict stoned or a suicidal person depressed, only one of their parts is drunk, mad, stoned or depressed. There is always another part which can be accessed. In the case of the alcoholic with an available metacommunicator, the easiest way to access the secondary sober state is to appeal to the available metacommunicator by telling him that he need not act drunk. You can even say to the metacommunicator, 'Stop acting drunk! Cut it out! Wake up and be sober! Let's deal straight with what is going on.' Note that you cannot do this with a psychotic person because during the acute episode there is no metacommunicator available who can help organize and access states. With a drugged person, however, accessing any secondary process when the primary one is drunk will be a very sobering experience because drunkenness is only a primary process. This knowledge was the motivating force behind the following interaction.

Herr G.:   My wife ran off the track. . . . It is true . . . she had no one to help her . . . I should have put her in a clinic . . . I knew . . . I knew her. . . . I knew it would not work . . . I knew that she would have exploded. I knew Ron, . . . it is no criticism of you that you did not help her.

Still keeping in mind that 'she' was the drunken part of him, I hoped a confrontation with him might produce an explosion, but might also bring about 'her' correcting 'her' life.

Arny: Herr G., *YOU* did not have the courage to tell her to enter a clinic. [Forcefully] *YOU* are the one who has failed her and who is now failing himself. So face this now!!

Herr G. looks upset. He drops his drunken appearance, opens his eyes wide open, faces me, and with one hand raised emphatically and operating in phase with his words, he increases his tempo and rhythm from a low tone to a crescendo, and says utterly soberly:

Herr G.:   I know that I did not have the courage. BUT NOW I DO HAVE THE COURAGE TO SAY THAT I DID NOT HAVE THE COURAGE THEN!

Regardless of the content of the conversation, I speak in the same raised tone of voice in order to bring out the sober state more:

Arny: NOW YOU HAVE THE COURAGE TO SPEAK.

Herr G. withdraws a bit, sits back in his chair and with a slightly lowered tone, disidentifies himself from the courage:

Herr G.: Is that courage? I have the courage today, but I did not have it when I needed it.

At this point Ron becomes like alcohol itself:

Ron: Herr G., relax. She was not unhappy or disharmonious on the day she died. I spoke with her on the phone. You could not have prevented her death, be realistic, Relax!

Herr G. gets angry. He increases his tempo and arches his back:

Herr G.: NO! You are not right!!

Another social worker breaks in angrily to Ron:

Social worker: Ron, what are you doing, what are you doing?

Ron reacts defensively, not to the question but to its implicit attack about not doing the right thing.

Ron: What am I doing? I am trying to tell G . . . we can talk to him . . . I am not his enemy.

What exactly happened here? Herr G. sobered up, became a bit more courageous and stopped acting like a failure. He found the courage to look closely and soberly at the fact that he was partly responsible for his wife's death. As soon as he became courageous and sober about his failure with his wife, Ron became the other side of the hologram again and said, 'Relax.' Telling him to relax polarized the situation again. Herr G. defended himself strongly and soberly, but his edge against his forcefulness was still there so he did not completely quieten Ron down. As a result, someone else stepped in and tried to do it.

ALCOHOLICS ANONYMOUS
One of the most successful drug therapies is Alcoholics Anonymous (AA). The somewhat evangelistic tone of AA works with many because it picks up on the alcoholic's secondary discipline and courage. Part of the program is for the AA member to claim, 'I am and always will be an alcoholic.' This statement mirrors Herr G.'s description of himself: 'I am a fool, and a failure.'

GOALS
Without understanding and following a given process structure, however, special methods such as AA are not necessarily successful because simply forbidding alcoholism uses only one part of the personality. There are many people with complicated processes who require more than escalating and accessing the courage and militarism in their secondary processes. They also need to find the meaning and the teleology in their drinking. Why was it a necessary thing for them? In Herr G.'s case, for example, the alcohol allows him, while acting drunk, to be less inhibited with his forcefulness towards others than he might otherwise be. In time, he needs to develop this courage with himself.

Many alcoholics will thus not be satisfied with simply resisting their tendency to drink and will want psychotherapy because only when they learn to follow their life process as a whole are they content. The above snapshot taken out of an interview is meant only as an indication of how to get along with a person in an intoxicated state. How far one must go with the alcoholic after having accessed the sober state is an individual matter depending upon the client and therapist.

THE FUTURE
It is possible to take a reasonable guess at what will happen
in the future or what could potentially happen by noticing
how close a client comes to the secondary process. The
following interaction gives me the feeling that Herr G. has
the potential to develop all sides of himself.

Arny: Herr G., I saw how you spoke a few minutes ago. I
was impressed. I now want to show you what I saw.
Take a good look at me now. You said [I act like G.,
using his gestures in order to anchor his courage], *I
do have the courage to act. Now I do have this courage
though I did not have the courage in the past.*
Herr G. (amazed and proud): Did I say that?
Arny: You did, and today you have the courage to give up
alcohol and today you have guilt feelings because
today, now, you are an alcoholic even though you
know that you have the courage to give it up.

Herr G. grins from ear to ear and clasps his hands in a
gesture of triumph.

Herr G.: Look. I am astounded by myself, by my own
courage. You know, I always had it.

Part V
THE CITY'S SHADOW

Chapter 12
THE SOCIOPATH

Paul exhibits some of the characteristics which would identify him as a psychopath, sociopath or an antisocial personality. According to the American Psychiatric Association's manual on mental disorders, a sociopath may be charming and of normal to high intelligence, though unreliable, untruthful and insincere. In addition, a sociopath usually lacks remorse for his acts and does not exhibit thinking characteristic of schizophrenia. 'Psychoneurotic manifestations' are lacking (Freedman et al,).

Sociopaths are usually, from earliest childhood onward, in conflict with their home life. Their childhood is typically disturbed and upset by alcoholic parents. They are incapable of loyalty to individuals, groups or social values. They are selfish, callous, irresponsible, impulsive and are usually unsusceptible to punishment. They tend not to feel love. They are rebellious and individualistic, but do not normally require institutional detention. As a whole, they tend to become more adapted during their forties. They rarely visit psychotherapists and come to the attention of the mental health profession through their conflict with the police and interactions with the social service agencies.

PAUL
Paul, at age thirty-nine, has a long record with the psychiatric and social work agencies because of his numerous interactions with the police. His file also mentions a heart attack and an attempted suicide. Because of his normal

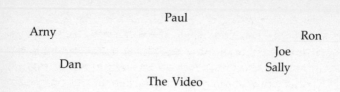

Figure 12.1   Paul's Circle

intelligence, his long history of conflicts with his family and his antisocial behavior, his earlier diagnosis would probably have been in the sociopathic range. Today, however, he is trying to reform.

As he walks in we see a solid, powerful-looking man with black curly hair, an open shirt, leather vest and a straight-forward, uninhibited way of relating. Paul has been addicted to various drugs, including heroin and alcohol. He is presently living in a clinic in an attempt to break his drug addictions. He says he is 'on leave' today in order to join us in our social work experiment.

As he speaks, Paul gives us the impression that he has been and still is the greatest drinker, fighter and musician in his village. His present process is somewhat the reverse of Herr G.'s in that Paul's present primary interest is in gaining insight, getting off alcohol and generally being 'good.' Sitting around the circle with Paul are Dan, Sally, Joe and I. Ron, who is Paul's social worker, is outside the circle, separated from Paul by about six feet.

Arny (to Paul):   Hi, how come you are visiting us today?
Paul: I am a patient in a clinic.
Arny: Why?
Paul (very loudly):   Because of drinking! Let me explain. I
    am an alcoholic.

Everyone in the circle laughs at his boldness and self-effacing nature.

Paul: Though I did not drink for awhile, it began again.
    Now I am in the clinic for treatment. Perhaps I will

get better, perhaps I will fall back into it again.

Dan: You have a long record of always getting into trouble, being in the middle of something all the time. Getting into fights, jealousy fits, gambling, losing your temper, getting picked up by the police for stealing, everything.

Paul: This is true. The problems I have now are the same as I had twenty years ago. I have not solved my problems. I run away from them.

Arny: What are your problems?

Paul: I have love problems for example. Yeah . . . that's a problem too! Twenty years ago I tried to shoot myself because of love troubles. Now I still have them. Later I had a lot of car accidents. I've always had accidents.

PROCESS STRUCTURE

Paul has a metacommunicator who discusses his various states. His primary process is to be 'a patient in a clinic,' identifying himself as an 'alcoholic' who has 'love problems and accidents' and who 'runs away from problems.' He is a 'cop', so to speak. What appears in his secondary process are violent car accidents, the police and a clinic. His secondary process is also to be an entertainer, as when he made us laugh by bragging about being an alcoholic. We can see this secondary process in his realism, when he states, 'perhaps I will get better, perhaps I will fall into drinking again.'

Paul: My parents never cared for us much. In early childhood my father wanted to take it easy and he and Mom did not pay much attention to us. The old man got remarried and changed for the better. All of us boys were wild and troublesome, so our mother had trouble with us. Especially since we always wanted to be the center of attention . . . my mother had trouble with us wild boys, poor woman. [Everybody laughs]

When Paul talks about the past, like all of us, he is dreaming, so to speak, in that he is compensating his present reality. Through stories of the past we all vicariously identify with secondary processes which we cannot or dare not live in the present.

In his present life, Paul is trying to reform and by doing so, he is the cop, the mother who tames his wildness. In his story of his childhood, his present secondary process appears in the form of a neglected child to whom no one pays attention, and thus the child is strong, wild and troublesome. He was and still is undoubtedly angry and wild about being neglected. The primary processes, embodied by the mother and also the police, are having trouble with the 'wild boys.' The authority in himself has little empathy for his neglected feeling situation.

Paul: I always wanted to be more than I was, but not today.
Arny: You mean today, too. Not even a little bit?
Paul: No, it is not good to want to be more than you are.
Arny (insisting):   But I want to be more than I am!

BRAGGING
It is obvious that Paul is dissociated from his bragging. He says, 'I always wanted to be more than I was, but not today.' He has split off the need to be the center of attention and therefore is not aware of how he grabs our attention. He does not appreciate himself enough.

To understand Paul's secondary process of wanting to be more than he is, remember a time when you have spontaneously bragged about something and then felt embarrassed about doing so. Do it now. Brag, claim that you are more than you are. Now see if you can find your edge against bragging. What stands in the way of your bragging? What have you got against it? When you have answered this question find out who you are now in the present moment in contrast to the part of you who bragged. The person who you are now is your primary process. The person who bragged is your secondary process which is already present, but which you do not want to identify with! Now let us look at Paul's secondary process and find out how to access it so he can use it consciously.

Paul: No, it is not good to brag.
Arny: But I want to be more than I am.

All the others speak up in agreement. It appears that everybody is having fun.

Paul (breaking in as the others enter the conversation): Well, naturally, I too want to be more than I am.
Arny: For example I wanted to show my son that I could somersault. And I did but almost broke my back doing it. How do you show you want to be more than you are?
Paul: If I could be more, I . . . was always able to entertain people with music. I had a local and popular little band, and we played all over town, in every restaurant and bar. Friday and Saturday nights. And in those days, I was very happy. I could do what others could not do. But then I got into a car crash and could not go on because of a paralysis. Then I changed. I tried to succeed in another way, I began to bluff. . . . For example I told people that I had a Mercedes instead of a bike. [Everyone laughs.] One should have insight. You should say that you don't have a Mercedes, only a bike. Earlier I would have said that I had a big car, even a Cadillac. It is not good, you should only say what you can do!

PROCESS WORK

How are we going to make him aware of his secondary process, his Mercedes Benz, his Cadillac? We are going to have to get around his negative mother who tells him he's a bad boy for bragging so much and needing to be the center of attention. The method I use here is to point out where he is a Mercedes now. I decided to show him how he is the center of attention and entertains us now, how he is powerful and will not let anybody enter the conversation. But since he was the center of attention, I had to wait, and then something interesting turned up.

Paul: About a year ago I had a heart attack. Around that time I had trouble with my girl friend, Mary. I myself always secretly wished that she would become, at that time, my wife and have kids with me. After five years, however, I realized that she did not want kids and that she had different life-style ideas than I. This made me [placing his right hand quickly on his chest] *kaputt*. I did not want to admit it but it did.

Arny: I noticed that you put your hand on your heart when you said you did not want to admit that she made you *kaputt*.

Paul: Yeah, you see, in our dialect, we say that if you are a troubled person (in German, *angeschlagen*, which means literally 'to be hit'), then your heart or soul . . . can . . . no longer go on.

One of the reasons love events are so disastrous is because the sufferer has an edge against feeling. The whole event is described in the past because though it is happening now, it is a secondary process. *Now* Paul is disturbed by a lot of things, now he is hurt by all sorts of problems but will not admit it. He is unconsciously acting like a tough guy, saying nasty things about himself, being hard and critical, and he does not admit that he is hurting himself. So right now, the pattern for the heart attack process is still going on. His mother, his primary and sober realism, is hurting the ordinary guy, the patient, his secondary process who has troubles. This is a common program for people with heart attacks.

TO DRINK OR NOT TO DRINK
Caring and loving himself, seeing that he is a powerful and sensitive guy is his core problem. His belief in himself as an

individual will determine whether or not he will get off
alcohol.

Paul: Without therapy . . . I may fall back into drinking.
Arny: How will this happen? I mean exactly?
Paul: That happens faster than you can know. Assume you
          are let out of the hospital. You get out, you go into a
          cafe to get a coffee. There you see an old buddy with
          other friends and their women. They invite you to
          celebrate a bit with them . . . they are drinking a lot
          but you have given it up. . . .
Joe: Let's act that out.

Everyone else in the room likes this idea and enters into the
scene. There is a lot of fun and laughter and generally a
good feeling.

Paul: Everybody's having a good time, they're happy, and
          I get angry. They have their drinks and I have my
          mineral water.

I move in closer to Paul to support him in his efforts to
resist.

Arny: I'll sit with you, man, I'm on your side.
Others (trying to lure him into drinking):   Come on Paul,
          have a drink!
Arny: Don't do it Paul.
Paul: Now, in the moment, you are here Arny, you're
          helping me. But if no one is there . . . a half-year
          ago, I would have told you, Arny, to leave. Today, I
          am no longer embarrassed by mineral water. I . . .
          I . . . I am no longer embarrassed.

He will probably return to drinking because he is embarrassed to drink mineral water, which means not being the kind
of man all the other guys are. The problem is that he does
not realize that he is important, central and worthy of
attention. Hence, he tries to be important in less useful

ways. He needs support in getting attention and in being himself. The next story shows this.

Paul: Years ago I got fed up with living with others in a therapy house. Everyone butts in, puts their noses in your business. Take my rabbits for example, I took care of them myself and bought, out of my own pocket money, their apples and lettuce and carrots. My money. But the others always put in their own two cents and said I should simply give them ordinary grass because the other food was too expensive. Of course, grass is also healthy. But I did not want to care for the rabbits like the others said, with only grass. I wanted to give them everything. I wanted to spoil my rabbits as if they were my wife, you know. I bought them all the best food. The others said I shouldn't. They drove me so mad that one day, I grabbed the rabbits, put them in a box, brought them to the butcher and said, 'Serve them in a restaurant!' I listened to the others. The pressure was too great. You can not do what you want when others are around.

Being an individual is very painful because it frequently goes against everything which the collective believes in. Most of us will throw away our most peculiar and individual personality traits if the pressure from without and the pressure from within to adapt is too great.

With Paul we still need to make him aware of the power he has to be himself when others are around, a power which is still secondary and which would make him a leader. The easiest way to do this is to point out how he is a leader and director now, with me, and with all of us.

ACCESSING THE LEADER
Arny: Bragging is not so bad.
Social worker (not understanding my approach): But Arny, being a bragger is not accepted as being a good thing.

Arny: But WHY does one brag?

Paul (interested): Yeah, that is a good question.

Arny: Let us say I brag that I have a Mercedes. I do this because I really am more powerful than I am presently acting. I am just afraid or unconscious of it. I am a powerful Mercedes now, I am not just a bike. Everything you say is somehow true.

Paul: Yes. I am a tough . . . in fact I am afraid of myself . . . I have no patience, I am afraid of myself. I am afraid of this power in my impatience. I could explode at any moment like (moving his arms explosively) – POW! –

If I were alone with Paul in my office, I would have worked with his nonverbal cue and have done body work with him. By gently resisting his arm motion which corresponded to 'POW,' I could have accessed his physical power. Such work is less adapted to the social work agency, however, than verbally accessing his power.

Arny: Yes! I see your powerful hand motions.

Paul (quickly): Wait till I am finished talking!

Arny: There it is, there is your power! [I was referring to his telling me to wait.]

Paul (breaking in again): Wait, I . . .

Arny (interrupting him): There is your power again.

Paul: Wait!

Arny: Here it is now!

Paul: Wait a minute. [Continuing his theme.] I always wanted to be more than I am.

Arny (raising my voice): Here you go again. You broke in.

Paul (ignoring me): Let me finish.

Arny (speaking quickly to get my message across): No. This is your power. You see, your power and impatience manifest themselves now in your ability to lead me around. This ability is your Mercedes. I wanted you to see it. I tried to get a word in edgewise, and you said, 'Be quiet.' Though you are supposed to be the patient you do not respect my

supposed authority as your doctor. I like this
powerfulness in you. This is the Mercedes. You are
not a bike [in a little tiny voice] you are no little
mouse. [Loudly] You are a powerful guy.

Paul: I do not understand.

Social Worker: Arny says you are a powerful guy in
directing.

Paul: Oh! Ah ha!

APPLYING INSIGHT

Insight alone is rarely enough, but needs to be experienced.
Paul needs not only to understand himself, but to feel his
leadership and power with us or in the outside world. The
next step would be to anchor this insight with experience.
Paul leads the way.

Paul: I have a question of my own. When I get out I'll need
a job. I'd like to be in your area Arny, in psychology.
I want to work in social stuff. I know that I must
have the strength to do it. But who will take me with
my sad record?

Instead of working with that part of him, his mother, who
does not take him seriously because he is or has been a bad
boy, I deal with his extraverted problem.

Arny: Me!

Paul (pausing): Thanks but I will need a job in three
weeks. In three weeks.

I think to myself that he is a great story teller, that he is very
visual and that his primary process is to get away from his
problems.

Arny: In three weeks you will need a job. Let us say that
you could create your own job. I know you can't.
But let us say you could. How would you do it?
How do you see yourself? Fantasy whatever you
want. Forget your present problems.

Paul (enthusiastically):   That's a good idea! Hmm. I would
   like to help young kids who do not know what to do
   with their lives. I would like to be responsible for
   them, to make a sort of home, to be a house father,
   give kids a place to live, something like Father W. I
   would like to care for kids to organize their eating,
   living. I feel responsible for them. But it is not
   possible for me to do this, not with my history.

Even though Paul is talking about his future, the problem in
the future is almost always present and approachable
through what he is doing right now with himself in the
moment. Right now he is trying to care for himself. His
secondary process, his father, mentioned earlier, is improving and taking care of the 'kids' more. Paul wants to be a
father, a spiritual leader, but first we must put the mother
aside.

Arny: Don't come back to your problems now. I will deal
   with them later. I am not interested in your past life
   now, but I want to know how you want to help
   others.
Paul: I could care for drug addicts, alcoholics, kids,
   jailbirds, people like me. For these people I want to
   be there. Yeah.
Arny: What a good idea! How can we do this?
Social worker: I think that this Father W. is really looking
   for helpers.
Paul: Yeah, I already help people. I brought two boys in
   last week for drug treatment. They like me. I used to
   be the biggest drinker in town. Twenty liters a
   morning. The kids respect me because I got off
   alcohol.
Joe: Call up now, show us who you are. Call up Father W.

Here is an example of why a team of social workers is better
in many respects than a single therapist or social worker. I
can understand process signals, but was uninformed about
job opportunities. The social worker compensates my

insufficient information. I need her and I need Joe who challenges Paul to put his power into practice. I did not think of calling Father W., but it was a good idea.

Paul goes over to the phone in the room.

Paul: Hello, Father W., this is a request concerning social
       work, about becoming a social helper.

INDIVIDUAL AND COLLECTIVE CONSIDERATIONS

Paul is right, this is a request about becoming a social helper. This interview concludes with a story book ending, with the hope that a poor guy with a painful and rough background turns good and helps others.

However, there is a subtle message in his story. From earliest childhood he did not have a warm, personal family. The city allotted him guardian parents through the social work agency. He has never been parented by a normal family system. But just this unusual situation is his fate, his process, his family. There are a lot of people from underprivileged homes who have suffered from rough conditions. But these people, seen from the process viewpoint, are not just underprivileged. They are children of the city. They belong to a larger collective commune, not to a personal, intimate family.

These troubled kids create and define the city as a family unto itself. Most of us have little awareness of this aspect of our cities. The city's kids are the ones who are alone or abandoned, who are outside of the nuclear-family paradigm. The city's kids are the ones no personal family can deal with. If the city's clients are its kids, then the entire mental health network becomes the parents of these children. This view of the social work network is a field concept and one which coincides with Paul's. A lot of therapists were, like Paul, simply kids who did not fit into their original and immediate surroundings.

Chapter 13
MENTAL RETARDATION

The American Psychiatric Association uses the terms 'borderline, mild, moderate, severe and profound retardation' to differentiate intellectual development under the normal IQ of 100. Borderline mental retardation ranges between an IQ of 68 and 85, while profound is 20 and under. The terms moron, imbecile and idiot, though obsolete, are still used to categorize subnormal intelligence, referring to adults with mental age levels corresponding to a child of eight, three to seven and three years respectively.

In England, the psychiatric profession classifies slightly subnormal and severely subnormal 'mental deficiency' where the IQ is less than 50 (Henderson and Gilespie, 1969). There, mental deficiency is differentiated from 'moral deficiency,' (the American 'sociopath') by the fact that the criminal or morally deficient person has a normal intelligence.

Subnormal intelligence due to known and unknown causes affects approximately 1 percent of the population. It is unusual for the psychotherapist in private practice to see this 1 percent. Though I have seen many in clinics in the last twenty-odd years of practice, I have worked with only four such individuals in my private practice. The mentally retarded person with an IQ of under 50 frequently requires supervision from a guardian or clinic and practically everyone in this category requires temporary help when faced with mild social or economic stress. The retarded person is usually kinesthetically oriented and performs poorly relative to others in verbal expression. Retardation may develop, be acquired through childhood diseases or be present at birth.

According to the American Association on Mental Deficiency, mental retardation refers to subaverage general intellectual functioning which originates in the developmental period and is associated with impairment in adaptive behavior. In addition, 'social maturation and learning are impaired.' Moderate retardation allows the individual to progress to between the second and sixth grade in academic subjects. Above the age of twenty-one the individual may achieve self maintenance in unskilled or semi-skilled work under sheltered conditions. The retarded adult often comes under supervision because of difficulties arising in relationship to city authorities, just as the retarded child commonly disturbs the rest of his class and his teacher as well.

EXPERIMENTING WITH RETARDATION
In order to understand Sam, the next client, it is important to see mental retardation as a state we can all, at one time or another, access. Imagine, for the moment, that you are retarded. What happens to you? Do you notice that your mouth and jaw relax? Have you noticed that you seem less alert than you normally are? What interests you and what do you want to talk about? Do you find that you are more interested in the basic things in life, like what to do next, who likes you, who doesn't like you, food, sex or money?

When was the last time you were mentally retarded? Are you retarded in the way you deal with love, money, sex, food and relationships? Do you recognize retardation as a state you are sometimes in when you are tired or overstressed? Do you sometimes act retarded instead of admitting that you are depressed or angry? As a retarded person, how do you behave when you are faced with strain or personal difficulties? Can you feel how much you want to be like everybody else and how sensitive you feel when you're not treated like others? If you can access your own retarded states, you will have more empathy and understanding for Sam who has a lot of troubles this morning.

SAM

Sam, now aged thirty, is the youngest of eight children and has suffered his whole life from his inferior intellectual and professional position in his family. Since he is not able to support himself, he has been a client of the social services for many years. He is not able to hold a regular unskilled job and has been receiving social security from the government. It seems that he can begin a job but then cannot attend the job regularly.

Our present meeting with Sam occurs under highly stressed conditions. He is running from the police. Moreover the entire interaction from the beginning emergency to the end solution took only fifteen minutes. He is fleeing from the home he has been living in after having got into a fight. The police are looking for him. In his confusion and nervousness, fear and unhappiness, he is seeking protection at the social service station where Jim, his guardian, is present. Sam is an emergency case this morning and is desperate.

Sam is already sitting when I get there. As I sit down I notice that he is very thin, weak and small looking. He has an unusually high pitched voice and stares at the floor unless talked to. He is dressed in an old suit jacket, like someone who wants to maintain a certain standing, though cannot quite afford it. When not directly spoken to, he drinks his coffee quickly and gobbles down a bunch of cookies. He is hungry and upset. I notice that his body gestures are more congruent, more stable and easier to understand than other types of people. He sits with a cigarette in his left hand while his right rests on his hip in an apparently aggressive position during the entire interview. His first sentences come out so quickly and emotionally that it was extremely difficult to understand him.

Arny: Hello, I am Arny.
Sam: I am Sam. [He looks down again after looking at me]
Arny (I turn to Jim and the others):   Why has he been
          rushed in here so quickly?

Jim: He is in a home, and did not hold out there. He ran
          away Saturday. He got into a mess. He did not
          know what to do. It is nice that he came to visit us
          here with his problems.

Arny (to Sam):   Is it bad there in the home?

Jim answers for Sam.

Jim: Yes, he did not know what to do.

Sam answers with such intensity and rapidity that it is
difficult to even transcribe from the tape, much less
understand him in person. His hand and arm motions are
more powerful than his words. It is obvious that he is
describing some powerful episode. Now, looking at me, he
says:

Sam: I can stand up for something. . . . Simply . . .
          something . . . went wrong . . . but . . . then . . .
          something has gone wrong . . . or, and . . . and to
          be . . . something . . . spoken about but that doesn't
          work.

EDGES

While looking at the tape without the intensity of the
moment it is clear that he has an unoccupied relationship
channel. 'I can stand up for something. Something . . . went
wrong,' . . . implies that something has happened to him in
a relationship which he did not create. Relationship
problems happen to him, thus we say that this channel is
not occupied.

He must have an edge (see Glossary) in that channel since
he formulates what he considers to be an impossibility:
'Speaking, talking things out . . . that doesn't work.' When
an edge appears, one way to deal with it is to test it directly
by saying (whether or not you know the issue), 'Of course it
works.' Locating the channel of a client's edge is an
important task since this is where their psychological
development lies.

I ignore the content of what Sam was trying to say because it was so difficult to comprehend, and relate instead only to the overall disturbance facing Sam.

Arny: It is nice that you came to talk. Sam, what sort of a state are you in, nervous?

Sam, in his excited and agitated state, did not pay attention to my exact question or was not able to understand the meaning of the concept of state, thinking 'state' meant 'place.'

Sam: It is not my place in the house, it is a place where . . . where one works, lives and eats. It is not my place. It is a worker's house.

I was still trying to make contact with him and therefore switched my theme to his, his 'home.'

Arny: Isn't it nice?
Sam: No, there are aggressive, nasty and addicted people there.

PROCESS STRUCTURE
Finally I begin to see some light in the mystery. Sam's primary process is to be an easy-going, decent fellow who feels a lot and who expresses himself kinesthetically. He claims he wants to talk things out and has trouble doing so. He dresses like a very sociable person.

His secondary process consists of the aggressive, nasty and unmannerly people in the house he is running from. His own aggression is obvious to me; I see his right hand on his hip while he is sitting, like a cowboy's posture. What exactly is this split off anger about?

Arny: Why do you live there?
Sam (shaking his head 'No'): People are there who did nasty things . . . came from other places. . . . [Changing the subject] . . . at the table I could not

take it any more, such disgusting asses at the table.
They act and eat terribly, throw stuff on the floor. I
left the table several times . . . and I had to leave.

Arny: How do they eat?

Sam: They throw stuff on the floor, not appetizing . . .
you know? Or they throw stuff . . . awful.

Because I could not understand Sam's story, I did not focus
on the content of what he was saying. I did not think of
those nasty guys as part of the world he has to learn to get
along with or as part of his process, his own aggression and
sloppiness.

Arny: But why are you there?

Sam: I was told it is the best place for me . . . ah . . .
oh . . . I was forced to go.

Arny: But why were you sent there, did you steal? Did you
hit someone? I would not live there even if they
forced me.

Sam (interrupting me in a moral and indignant tone): Before
I hit, I always talk to people!

EXAMINING MY OWN BEHAVIOR

As I transcribe the interview I notice that I appear to be
confused about what Sam is saying. As a result I miss the
relationship issue, i.e. with whom is he fighting? Instead, I
search for my own grounding, ignore the information in
front of me, and then do something which is probably very
typical for people around Sam. I talk about him with the
others as if he were not there or not capable of taking part in
the conversation.

Sam accepts this passively, without realizing that he is
being treated as if he were absent. Being constantly ignored
is very humiliating and hurtful to him as it would be to
anyone. Though he does not refer to our present interaction,
later in the interview he tells me that it was awful being the
youngest and the most handicapped of eight kids, the one
who was never able to learn a normal profession and who
was always neglected by the others.

THE HYPERACTIVITY OF THE RETARDED

Hyperactivity in small children and aggression in later life is due, in part, to being ignored and neglected. Much hyperactivity is concealed anger and humiliation. Though he is an adult, Sam is treated like a child. This treatment is an insult to him, though he does not consciously realize it. His aggression, therefore, is a defense against the insult. The above interaction shows us that he does not identify with being a nonverbal, kinesthetic person. 'Before I hit, I always talk to people!' means that affect and aggression overtake him, partly because he has trouble discussing things and needs to learn to express anger verbally.

To avoid neglecting and ignoring the retarded person because he does not relate in a verbal mode, it is necessary to understand his communication. Sam's feelings and movement are, in some senses, more developed than other people's. An 'intelligent' communicator (no such person was present in the situation at hand!) will learn to switch channels and relate with motions and emotions. Most of us do not naturally possess this communication intelligence and will have to learn it. My recommendation is that we video tape all interactions with unusual clients in extreme states in order to learn from them how to communicate nonverbally.

WORKING WITH SAM

If I had the time to work in depth with Sam (I could not because there was another emergency at the agency that day), I would show him that we ignore him partly because he passively accepts being discussed and does not press us to understand his feelings better. I would tell him that his apparent intelligence defect could be due to the fact that his emotions need more expression. If they are kept back, they disturb his ability to concentrate and think.

In order to get this point across, I would ask him if he gets upset when people mistreat him. If he said no, I would deliberately and provocatively ignore him in order to elicit his awareness of how he lets people walk over him. If he succeeds in getting angry at me when I irritate or ignore him, I would then help him verbalize his anger with me, right there and then. Or, on the other hand, I might tell him to have greater pride in himself. He should not only wear a nice jacket, but should increase his self-esteem completely.

His task would be to stop us, ask what we are talking about, and tell us if he does not understand. He should make certain that we do what he wants to do. And if we don't, he will have to learn to stand up for himself. To help him learn this, I would actually move him, as I have done with other such people, to a corner of the room and then deliberately neglect him in order that he physically experiences the feeling of being left out. If he does not learn to defend himself he will do it unconsciously in a non-constructive way like a fight, which may cost him his relationship to people who are meaningful to him.

Returning now to the interview, we see how relationship problems constitute his central issues.

Arny: Do you have family?
Sam: My family is in Biel.

Apparently a big complex has been constellated here, for Sam puts his hand on his head and pushes his hair back. The social workers, who apparently know more about his family history than I, move about uncomfortably.

Sam: I have to tell you an example, I called my father the other day. He was in agreement. My brother is a bit . . . greedy for money . . . married . . . ah . . . married a rich girl. . . . I get along well enough with the old man, but the brother . . . [raising his voice] when the old man is not there, my brother holds or grabs everything for himself. And with eight kids . . . well . . . he is greedy [showing me the brother's greed with his hands] greedy, greedy.

Sam gulps down another cup of coffee and gobbles up a few more cookies. I decide to aim now for the secondary process:

Arny: Yes, HE can get what he wants. If we knew how he did that then we could apply that pattern now.

I am thinking symbolically, hoping to access Sam's own greed and power, so that he will not be dependent upon the social services and the rest of the world for money. But my track is interrupted by a social worker who does not understand my intentions.

Social worker (to Sam): Now, getting back to the situation at hand. Are you sad?
Sam: Yes, I am . . . it hurts, deeply . . . down to the bone. It costs . . . I notice. . . .

I let go of my interest in his brother and adapt to the overall situation.
Arny: When you first came in here, you were so nervous. How come you now feel better?
Sam: I felt uneasy, I could not sleep. I felt pinned in as if I had done the stupidest thing, as if I had done the worst thing or had been a criminal.

Apparently he feels better because we have accepted him as a person, but the problem is still here, it is in the background, in the past ('I felt uneasy'). The relationship conflict is still present because one of his hands is still on his hip, cowboy style, waiting for what, I ask myself.

Arny: You need friends . . . good friends.
Sam: I have a buddy. I do not know where he is now. Another friend invited me for a two-week trip to Spain.
Arny (to the others): I would like to see him with one of these friends. He needs to work on his relationships.
Sam: I have a girl friend. But she is divorced, has a big apartment. She got kids. Been there twice, nice girl, like her.
Arny: Could you bring her once with you?
Sam: Well, I don't know. . . .

Social worker: Arny, what do you mean by relationship?
Sam: It is like this . . . it is like this . . . to make a
friendship [taking his hand from his hip to express
himself fully], you have to fight for it. It is always
that way. . . .

ON RELATIONSHIP

Two very interesting aspects of the work are evident here.
First, the concept of relationship is missing in this social
work center. Relationship for me is learning how to process
the communication which is present. It does not mean
securing a permanent or necessarily harmonious contact
with someone. The relationship which the social worker and
the client have in mind is state or role oriented, having
someone there who is your friend, in contrast to process
oriented; being aware of and working with what happens to
yourself when you are with others.

The second interesting aspect of the above conversation is
that Sam tells us that to have a relationship you must be
prepared to fight. His primary process is not ready to stand
for anything or to fight. His secondary process, like his
brother, will grab whatever he needs. Fighting for what he
wants has been the missing element in relationships until
now.

How can we bring this out? We could either constellate a
fight now with us or return to the place of his problems and
work there. In the following interaction, both were
attempted.

LEARNING TO FIGHT

Arny: What is the problem there in the home? What is the
real problem in the outer world?
Sam: For me it is . . . it could be good . . . for people
who . . . for example . . . there were many
reasons . . . for alcoholics, when they have money
in their pockets. . . .
Social worker: He has too high requirements for his
environment.

Sam: NO! THAT I HAVE TO DISAGREE WITH YOU
ABOUT!!! THAT IS NOT TRUE. When there are
people there who have money, they go drinking.
Alcoholics. They disturb me. I don't need them.
How do you get along with them?

I notice that his fighter is beginning to come out as he resists
the social worker, but I am hoping to locate the relationship
problem where the present situation began.

Arny: Who is the person who hurt you? Who hurt you?
Sam: I know. . . . Everyone has troubles. Everyone blames
others.
Arny: I will not tell anyone. Who hurt you?
Sam: Yeah. . . .
Arny: Who?
Sam: I must be. . . . [mumbling quietly to himself].
Arny (warmly but forcefully): Who? Who did it?
Sam: Well, . . . well . . . the boss. If you work they are
happy, they like you.
Arny: What did he do?
Sam: He says . . . each . . . the boss looks at you like
cattle, you feel locked in, like pinned in, you are like
locked in there.
Arny: I want absolutely to talk to him. A relationship
problem, I want to talk to him. Sam runs into
relationship trouble, and then runs from his problems, because he feels too weak . . . like all of us.
Sam (spontaneously): No, it is not just that. For example
with housekeeping. The thing I cannot take is, the
room is checked at 9.30. Like in military, no worse.
No alcohol, no alcohol, no drinking. I don't like
being controlled. But if I see that the boss is in the
cafe and is drunk, then, when he comes home and I
see him . . . yeah. He comes back, then I would get
really angry . . . I would like to slap him. Yeah, it is
simply unfair. [He lights a cigarette]
Arny (to the social workers): You will have to stand in
between him and the boss of the home and mediate,

help them both process what is happening.

Sam: The boss in not fair.

Social worker: But the problem of keeping the house in order is still there. He needs to be orderly, no?

Arny: True, but this is not just a personal problem, it is a relationship problem as well. It has to do with how he behaves at the moment when others bother him. And this is where he is at the moment. If he solves this relationship issue, then he can work on the next. But at the moment it seems as if his disorderliness is an unfinished battle against those in himself and in the world around him who treat him poorly.

Jim: That's right. He has the same problem all over.

Social worker: Tomorrow, when we see the head of the home, what shall we do?

Sam (apparently afraid of this new thing):   OK. If it's so bad, and nothing else works, then I will return to the home. (Now very angrily, using both hands.) Do you think it is nice to be put down? It hurts to always be at the end of things, to be at the bottom. Do you think it is nice to be at the bottom of eight kids, and the smallest and the one with the least skills? Do you think that is nice?

I agree with Sam that it must have been awful for him to be the last of eight kids and the one with the fewest skills. But I also think that it must be terrible for him constantly to identify himself as the weakling who only notes the injustice in the past. Why does he dwell on his stories about the past? As we saw in earlier chapters, things which happened in the past are experienced as unchangeable; they become part of our fate, an unalterable myth or pattern, frozen into the glaciers of time. Thus the reference to past events indicates that Sam experiences the present as a hopeless and inevitably unjust situation. He needs help not only externally but internally as well with his hopelessness about becoming a strong and independent person.

THE MEANING OF RETARDATION FOR THE CITY

I also think, however, that Sam's present inferior position in our culture makes him and others like him all the more sensitive to the governing authorities in a given community. One of the teleological meanings of retardation for the individual is, as it is with all handicaps, to learn to stand up for and appreciate oneself as an original and individual creation.

But as long as Sam cannot do this, he is dependent upon others for help. His problems dream the social services into being; they create the need for the city's agencies. And these agencies in turn create networks which must deal with Sam and with difficult and painful problems, such as Sam's home director whom no one but the retarded person fully experiences. In other words, because the *retarded person* is less able than others to rationalize his feelings away, he *becomes the city's sensitivity towards its own insensitive behavior.*

In Sam's case, it turned out that the director of the home was a highly disturbed alcoholic who needed someone to stand up to him and to force him to change. Sam was the warning signal indicating that all was not well and that he and others were being maltreated. Working with people like Sam inevitably means working with the community and its leaders. In a case like this, as in all cases, social psychiatry must widen its reach and work with all aspects of the community situation.

Chapter 14
THE CITY'S SHADOW

The foregoing process studies of schizophrenia, mania, depression, heroin and alcohol addictions, mental retardation and sociopathy are only part of the immense topic of extreme states. Missing from the present study are investigations of senile psychoses, extreme states in children and comatose phenomena near death.

The client of the city often appears to be the identified patient of the community; he channels its repressed and unrealized psychology. This shadow is like the city's dream portraying its neglected gods, the hopelessness it will not admit, its withdrawal from superficial communication, its suicidal tendencies, mania, addictions, murderous rage and hypersensitivity. The shadow reminds us of the smoldering revolution we normally perceive only in the dark of night or in the impinging quality of physical symptoms.

None of the above 'diseases' appears to be purely random or meaningless pathological behavior; each shows, in all situations, a highly ordered, almost mathematical predictability. One goal of this work has been to demonstrate that the cause-and-effect, illness-and-cure philosophy governing much of psychiatric research and treatment is not the only useful way of either observing or treating the effects of the above syndromes. A process oriented paradigm which studies the various channels of human expression and which deals concretely with both individual and collective issues, normal and extreme states, is sorely needed. The

The Client

Client's Family		The Neighbors
Psychologist		Analyst
Psychiatrist		Social Worker
Psychiatric Researcher		Psychological Researcher
Medical Doctor		Psychiatric Nurse
City Authorities		Courts
Police		Insurance Agencies

The City

Figure 14.1   The mental health team

new paradigm blends psychiatry with social work, psychology and politics.

The mental health professions of the future will, I imagine, see our present psychiatry, psychology, social work, medicine and politics as specialized and divided approaches to extreme states and social and physical problems. One way of bringing these specialized professionals together today is to see them as one team. This team looks approximately as shown in Figure 14.1.

TO THE ANALYST

In my opinion the analyst should be a model of understanding and flexibility in modes of treatment for other mental health disciplines. However, most analytical interventions are only weakly applicable to psychotic states. It is possible that there are basic assumptions in the way you, the analyst, practice which are limited to normal psychology and which do not apply to extreme states.

If you find that your work does not apply to the psychotic states, you normally conclude that the people are unconscious and must wait for enlightenment. Secretly you believe that humankind will never change. You are hopeless. Alternately, you may believe that psychosis is due to social ills, God, the collective unconscious, an undiscovered toxin, early childhood experiences or fatefully weak egos.

These beliefs indirectly help to sustain the steady number of psychotic episodes because you, who are best trained to work with these people, defer such work to others. Moreover, your hopelessness acts hypnotically on patients in extreme states by intensifying their own anger and sense of hopelessness. Please let us be aware of our beliefs about psychotic states.

TO THE PSYCHOLOGIST

Psychotic states are process reversals in which secondary processes are exchanged for primary ones for more than a short duration. Everyone has such altered states; hence, psychosis is just one end of a spectrum of states. At one end is consciousness and awareness, while at the other there is literally no control. Everyone's psychotic corner can be accessed by touching upon a central, mythical, painful issue.

An important characteristic of altered states is that many of them cannot be sufficiently dealt with without entering them. For example, consider a man who complains that he is troubled by anxiety attacks which he says, upon questioning, make him 'flutter.' Normally, he says, he is a very sensitive and delicate person, but not anxious. His 'normal state of mind,' that is, his primary process, is to be sensitive, cool and unafraid, his secondary one is to flutter.

We can remain in our primary process and talk to him, encouraging him to remain in a normal state but the chances of our getting at the core of his anxiety and relieving it are not very great. To deal directly with his present problem we might, for example, encourage him to get into that altered state, into his secondary process by using the 'fluttering' as a signal characteristic of this state. When he begins to flutter, he visualizes a figure threatening him. Then suddenly he tells us that he is afraid his father will strangle him! Now he automatically comes out of the altered state.

He seems his normal self again. He tells us that while in that state he realized that he has preferred to repress his own voice rather than be forceful with others. The insight obtained from the experience, that being forceful is difficult for him, coupled with the fact that the fluttering stopped when he began to be more forceful, leads us to wonder why talking about his 'negative father complex,' that is, about the way he represses himself, did not help him. It seems as if one solution to his anxiety problem lay hidden in the complete experience of an altered state and therefore occurred in switching states and processes, in accessing the fluttering and finding out more about its nature.

Only a few of the problems people suffer from can be dealt with by remaining in this reality. The solutions to most problems require wisdom and experience of altered states. We need to learn how to switch realities fluently, how to be able to transport information back and forth between an altered state and a normal primary process. I think that the biggest problem we have working with psychotic episodes is therefore connected to our inability to define, access and switch realities, to remain in one while carrying information from another. So let's learn!

TO THE BIOMEDICALLY ORIENTED PSYCHIATRIST
What are our basic assumptions behind ameliorating psychotic effects? We should check our desire to medicate *all* extreme states, otherwise we propagate an inadvertent form of communism, a collective ban on abnormality. We know that there are many individuals suffering in extreme states whose processes are potentially mind expanding, whose behavior is highly critical of western technological society and who, given the proper help, could be constructive culture changers. Some may even become future therapists.

If we medicate such people, we may be avoiding our own myth of truly helping. Are we giving medication because it is really the process of the individual or are we sometimes giving it because we no longer want to think about the complex situation of our patient or about the basic premises of our profession?

Paradigm Revolution
Being a psychiatrist today means being part of a revolution in medicine. Psychiatry, more than any other branch of medicine, is faced with the limitations of causality. As a

student you once challenged the basis of your profession; its flaws confront you no less glaringly today.

A central term in psychiatry is 'psychosis.' In this text psychosis is defined as a process reversal without a metacommunicator. The primary process which was originally adapted to a given family or community is, for a number of reasons, reversed with the secondary process long enough to change the way in which the individual experiencing the reversal is observed by others. Instead of a primary process which is adapted to the reality in which one lives and which is periodicially disturbed by a secondary process, we have a new and surprising primary process which is unrelated to the consensual reality and disturbed by reality orientation.

The definition assumes that the individual in an extreme state experiences a highly patterned process and that psychosis is one of many processes characterized by temporary process reversal. This definition requires you to be aware of your own state of awareness and that of your city. It also demands knowledge of the individual client's idiosyncratic messages and signals.

This definition has cross-cultural applications as well, since it examines the individual's feeling, thinking and relationship to the world independently of their cause. Specific western terms for an extreme process such as schizophrenia may now be compared with apparently analogous disease entities defined in other cultures (cf.Kiev, 1973), since all psychoses are reversals of a culture's primary process.

Thus, if law and order, cleanliness, tidiness and hard work are characteristic of a given culture, a person will be psychotic if he tends, for a long period of time, to be unlawful, disorderly, unclean, untidy and lazy. In a culture where intuitiveness is accepted, fantasy is not likely to be considered a symptom of disease.

Polarization
Defining psychosis as a process reversal and as an unusual or extreme state implies that the client's ability to exist in a

given environment is disturbed. This means that the psychiatrist has to be acutely aware of her client's resistances to the world and also of her own resistances to the client, for process reversal polarizes the environment. The world around an individual in the midst of a process reversal always becomes her opposite, just as the client becomes the secondary process for the world. Without understanding what is happening, a therapist usually finds herself acting out the opposite part of a client's pattern, the cop to the robber, the optimist to the depressive and so on, instead of making both processes more accessible to the client.

If the therapist becomes antagonistic to the patient's state, both are in for trouble. Creative work with an extreme state requires you to be outside the state and outside of its polar opposite, while simultaneously getting inside and fully empathizing and appreciating it. But the latter is only possible when you are not caught in it.

The psychiatrist is faced with many unanswered questions. Why is one client susceptible to one type of process reversal rather than another? Our knowledge at present indicates only how patients become psychotic and how to deal with them. We know that individuals with weak primary processes become schizophrenic under stress, in contrast to becoming physically ill. Individuals with strong primary processes, on the other hand, become psychosomatically ill and experience process reversal as a temporary fever or debilitating handicap. Where there is an edge against violence, epilepsy is common. The following hypothesis needs testing as well; people attached to a primary process of peace become addicted to drugs or endorphine effects such as those produced by physical exercise. What kinds of belief systems are present before the onset of catatonic states? Can retardation be altered through processing?

Prediction
One problem which you are often faced with is predictability. You will be asked to predict which people are likely

to be dangerous to others and to themselves, and then have to make decisions based on those judgements. The process paradigm, at this early stage, offers a few notes about this. Clients with no edge to their secondary processes will follow these processes with little or no hesitation. For example, someone who says, 'Others have killed themselves. Why not me?' is in dangerous trouble. A congruent primary message without double signals is also believable. 'I will kill myself soon,' without any superfluous or contradictory body motions is a serious statement. The best way I know of dealing with these situations is to believe them and help the individuals play, imagine or fantasize these situations now, as if they were happening in your office. In this way, dangerous situations can turn into constructive ones.

TO THE SOCIAL WORKER
Some of you have already had a lot of training in managing medical and city authorities. I will therefore address others who might need a greater overview and additional support for their work.

You are required to be part psychiatrist, part analyst, part business and economic expert, family therapist, and mediator between the courts, the family and the taxpayer.
Your role is full of problems! You frequently feel inferior in training and importance to the psychologists and psychiatrists you work with and feel that your position is not respected enough. And you are right, but this is partly your

Social team conflict

clinic	:	guardians
doctor	:	social agencies
police	:	family
courts · · · · · · · · · · · · · social worker · · · · · · · · · · · · · client
city government	:	the client's boss
debtors	:	family
neighborhood	:	relatives

your inner problems.

Figure 14.2 The social worker's position

own doing. Many of you did not want to submit yourselves to the long and arduous training offered to analysts, psychiatrists and psychologists. But perhaps you were right; some of the training is not really as useful as it could be! Why not define the problems of your profession better and seek the kind of training you need, training which will bridge the gaps between individual psychology and city problems?

I recommend that you redefine your role. In Figure 14.2, your position relative to the world around you is schematically portrayed. Your job is a mixture of all the abilities needed in the client's situation, as well as the ability to switch roles as the situation demands. Since your job deals with the entire city you are like a mind in the midst of a body. A problem in one part of the body demands that you make contact with that part and examine the entire situation surrounding it. As a general rule, the organization of the entire body must change so that the troubled part improves.

Your client is the city's 'identified patient,' the part identified as being ill or troublesome. But the city's tendency to identify him will also have to change, in the same way the family who identifies one of its members as a problem has to change. In other words, *both the individual client and the city are your clients*. Both your individual client and your city are in the midst of change. What a difficult, impossible and exciting job!

You are going to have to mediate the relationship conflict between the restaurant manager who threw out your alcoholic client and the client himself. You will have to help him with his neighbors and them with him. You will have to interact with the police and with the courts who accuse your client of stealing and who implicate you for refusing to give him more money to continue his habit. You must bargain with the store owner who wants immediate compensation for the stolen property and with your client who is unable to come up with the compensation. You are working not only with your client's personal psychological problems, but with the restaurant's role in creating addiction, the policeman's brutality, the store owner's vindictiveness and the clinic director's private problems.

The city requests you to keep the client out of trouble and under the rug. Consider yourself part of a city that expects you to be a trash collector responsible for hiding the wastes, that disregards the human consequences and disasters resulting from this attitude. You get the person nobody else can deal with. Knowing that your present role is often subtly defined as the city garbage dump may help you change this situation. Your experience has political implications. No one knows better than you the total story around heroin and sociopathy. Who else could inform the city about the life of an alcoholic?

The court can no longer pass their problems on to you, it will have to learn to have it out with the client. Tell the court about how they and the client blackmail you! How they threaten you with not giving the client his social security. Tell them that being tough with a client in a given moment may risk a burglary but may also finally solve a problem which has been hanging on for years. Tell them that the garbage dump is overloaded, it cannot take any more and that the public is going to have to learn to process the difficulties faced by the social services.

The Staff Problems

To deal with the city's problems, you will have to work on the internal tension which is characteristic of all mental health staffs. Though this seems to be adding more problems to your agenda, working on staff tensions will improve your working atmosphere and your ability to deal with difficult clients. For many cases are so complicated and troublesome that you need others to help you with your work. Don't try to handle impossible situations alone.

Find as many helpers, trained and untrained, as you can. You may need to work in teams of three, four or five at a time. If you need more time or money to do this, you should fight for it, claiming that getting one client off the streets saves the city a lot more money than it costs to hire more helpers. A financial investment with the potential of saving in the future is a wise one.

TO THE CITY GOVERNMENT
Each year you must pay city officials, social agencies, state agencies, insurance funds, police and tax losses to support the kinds of clients mentioned in this work. Instead of trying to maintain the status quo and implying that your social services should keep the shadow quiet because the tax-payers want this, consider the following. The shadow destroys cultures if it is not valued and its meaning not understood. Intensive care for the city shadow would mean learning about it and publicizing both its financial costs to the city and its message from another world about the future of our planet. Some of its present messages seem to be:

1 *Trance states are important*
Introversion is not a disease, but a corner of the personality waiting to be experienced by everyone. Not everyone needs to talk. Look into trances, examine them. In these states, the world itself is stopped and reconsidered.

2 *The gods are still around*
The city's shadow shows that the archetypes of the Virgin Mary, Napoleon and Jesus are still around, though nobody takes much interest in them these days. Fantasy is important, for it teaches about the totality of being human. These savior figures and god-like experiences are channeled through the shadow because they are not welcomed by the collective. You don't believe in these figures because you do not know yourself yet.

3 *The shadow is a trickster*
A message of the city's shadow is to relax. It is important to be retarded sometimes, not to think but to focus only on feeling problems which everyone else skips over. The shadow is a trickster because it says that it is always time for vacation, time for more sex and fun. The shadow says to brag more, because by

bragging we see parts of ourselves we do not take seriously now. The shadow says a good fight in the best of families sometimes clears the air. The city shadow says that we are crazy, the shadow is the healthy one.

The shadow wants to be cared for. He says, 'I am not interested in pain. I have no courage and am not a hero in life like you. I give up on life, I sometimes need to collapse, even commit suicide. I am sometimes a slow and timid outsider, won't you wait for me? I have troubles. I am old, senile, sick and suffering and cannot make it alone. I am mad, addicted, violent, lonely and homeless. I have fits of jealousy and feel betrayed. You know me in yourself!'

TO THE CLIENT

I know that you suffer from feeling unwanted. You are the identified patient of a troubled world family. We contribute to making you believe that you are a useless failure and I know that you secretly feel that life is not for you. You are partially correct when in your altered states you perceive that this world is in trouble and that you are in order. Your life could show us the dreaming element in the world yet we dwell upon categorizing you. While we maintain the threads of history, you thieves, bag ladies, gods and holy people spin the eternal present.

Your living demon frightens us and we try in vain to turn away. For when we see your unthinkable visage we remember that part of ourselves which is connected to the wonder of life. Why don't you realize that we are both inflexible; both think the other is crazy, both feel unrelated to and incapable of relating. Both feel despised. Both of us are asleep. Who will wake up first?

GLOSSARY

In the following Glossary, psychiatric definitions are related to process concepts. This Glossary is neither complete nor definitive, but is meant to aid the reader in understanding certain sections of this work without having to refer to other texts on the subject of process work.
*preceding a word indicates that it is defined elsewhere in the Glossary.

Addiction
Conflict between a *primary and a *secondary process in which one uses increasing quantities of a drug to support a secondary process in order to overcome the primary one. Typical drugs are morphium, heroin, alcohol, cigarettes, coffee and tea.

Affect
Overwhelming secondary emotion which partially or totally submerges the *primary process.

Alcoholism
An *addiction to alcohol.

Altered states
A term referring to a *state of *consciousness which is different from the state connected to *collective primary process. For example, if ordinary waking consciousness is our primary state, altered states include nocturnal dreaming, hypnotic conditions, drunken and drugged states, states centered around strong emotions like rage, panic,

depression, elation, or states induced by meditation.

Archetypes

The implicit structure and organization of *processes which may appear in dreams, body problems, relationships, *synchronicities and hallucinations.

Computer Aided Tomography (CAT) Scanning

X-rays of brain structures formed by the difference in x-ray absorption from the fluid in the ventricular spaces and the brain tissue itself.

Channel

The specific mode in which information is received, for example, the visual, auditory, proprioceptive, kinesthetic relationship and world channels refer to information picked up respectively by seeing, hearing, feeling, moving, through another person or an outer event.

Collective primary process

This is a consensus reality, a *primary process shared by the majority of individuals in a given family or community. This process simulates the world and the environment. A *psychotic person no longer shares this picture of reality. This process resembles the primary process of an individual, except that instead of 'I', which an individual uses to refer to his role in a given collective, he uses 'we,' by which he refers to a primary process shared with others.

Collective unconscious

A term developed by Jung referring to experiences which are found among people from all over the world. These experiences are symbolized in dreams by figures without immediate personal associations from one's past such as kings, queens, magicians, trees, animals, etc. The collective unconscious frequently appears in *secondary processes.

Complex

A term originally defined by Jung which in this work refers to a disturbance of attention due to a *secondary process which has been accessed and disturbs the stability of the *primary process. The complex is organized by an *archetype, has an awareness of its own and structures a given secondary process.

Consciousness
This term refers to having an observer who can *meta-communicate and who is aware of the mode and channel in which perception is occurring.

Depression
A *state of great unhappiness in which one's tempo of speech and movements are slowed down. It can become a *psychosis if there is a reversal of the original *primary and *secondary processes. There is, except in psychotic cases, a *metacommunicator present who is able to communicate with others.

Dreaming Up
This expression refers to the phenomenon which occurs when a *double signal creates reactions in another person. The term comes from the empirical observation that the reaction in the other person is always reflected in the double signaller's dreams.

Double signal
Language or body gestures which the communicator does not identify with. Signals or communication which are related to a *secondary process.

Dreambody
The phenomena which occur when body experiences which have been *secondary are amplified creating an *altered state of consciousness which mirrors one's dreams.

Edge
The experience of not being able to do something, being limited or hindered from accomplishing, thinking or communicating. Structurally speaking, an edge separates the *primary from the *secondary process.

Endogenous
Coming from or occurring within.

Epilepsy
A group of symptoms characterized by the sudden and temporary loss of the *primary process. One suddenly loses awareness, either by falling asleep or into a stupor, losing control of speech and body movements, etc. In 'petit mal' seizures, speech and actions may simply be interrupted briefly or the person may drop something.

'Grand mal' seizures involve repeated, uncontrolled, violent clonic movements of all the muscle groups. The person may be injured in thrashing about or may bite the tongue. Subjectively, a seizure may typically be experienced as being thrown to the floor or possessed by an alien spirit.

Exogenous
Coming from or occurring without.

Extreme states
*States which are normally antagonistic or unusual in a given community, for example, a *psychotic episode or *altered state of consciousness.

Feedback
A response occurring as a reaction to a given stimulus.

Feedback loop
The chain of reactions in which a stimulus signal receives and is altered by *feedback. There is no feedback loop in many *extreme and *psychotic states.

Field
A feeling of causal or acausal interconnectedness between various places or people, and evidence for the existence of such interconnectedness as in the case of *synchronicity.

Global dreambody
Two or more people together with their environment considered to function as a body whose *processes, body gestures and outer *synchronicities mirror their dreams.

Grower's club
A jovial way of describing the kinds of people and *processes in which there are *metacommunicators interested in integrating *primary and *secondary processes.

Hologram
A concept borrowed from physics which describes the behavior of parts and the whole. Each part carries the same patterns as the original whole.

Illness
Subjective experience of being disturbed by a *secondary process.

Individuation process
This term was originally defined by Jung and refers to the

life-long development of an individual capable of integrating all of the various parts of the personality into ordinary life. In process thinking, individuation also refers to the ability to access any *altered state, such as a dream figure, body problem or relationship projection and to live and process these states in the moment they are present without losing contact with one's ordinary identity.

Mania
Wild excitement usually connected to identifying with a *secondary process which disturbs the environment while still being capable of communicating with it.

Medical model
According to this model of *extreme states, malfunctioning of the brain causes mental disorders and requires pharmacological intervention. This model is based upon the discovery that various physical and mental processes are controlled by different parts of the brain and that certain chemicals affect electrical transmission in the neural network.

Mental illness
An *illness without known chemical causes in which behavior does not conform to the norm of a given community.

Mental retardation
Subnormal intelligence accompanied by emotional difficulties and a sober-minded *metacommunictor who requests supervision and assistance with daily life.

Metacommunication
The capacity to communicate about the content and process of communication.

Neurosis
Any long-lasting experience in which a *metacommunicator experiences his *primary process as being endangered or overcome by a *secondary one.

Occupation
The process of relating to or identifying with one of the parts or *states of a *process. For example, visualization is not occupied if we say that others look at us and we are unaware of our own active looking. Or a man's father is

not occupied if he dreams of the father and projects it onto the outside world.

Personal unconscious
A term defined originally by Jung. The *primary process of a person in consensus reality. This process is usually symbolized in dreams by known figures identified with one's past.

Positron emission tomography
A neurotransmitter analog in which one of the atoms is replaced by an isotope (a positron emitter) and given to a patient to see where the drug is and how it combines while the patient is alive.

Primary process
The body gestures, behavior, and thoughts with which one identifies oneself or which it can be assumed one would identify with if asked.

Process
The flow of signals and of information as defined by those who perceive it. Process is differentiated into *primary and *secondary information which is closer to or further from the sender's awareness.

Psychiatry
The study and management of *extreme states.

Psychosis
In process terms, psychosis is the process in which an earlier *primary process is exchanged and becomes secondary while the earlier *secondary process becomes primary. This process occurs without a *meta-communicator and lasts for more than several weeks.

Psychotic corner
A *psychotic process of relatively short duration such as a week or two. Everyone has psychotic corners.

Schizophrenia
A *psychosis in which there is no *metacommunicator present and which has minimal *feedback loop with the content of communication.

Secondary process
All the verbal and nonverbal signals in an individual's or community's expressions with which the individual or

community does not identify. The information from
secondary processes is usually projected, denied, and
found in the body or outside the sender.

Shadow
A term originally defined by Jung to mean a dream figure
of the same sex as the dreamer which symbolizes or
'personifies everything that the subject refuses to acknow-
ledge about himself' which nevertheless thrusts 'itself
upon him directly or indirectly.' It is, 'for instance, inferior
traits of character and other incompatible tendencies.'
(Collected works vol. 9, Part 1, pp. 284–5.) Depending
upon the state of the individual and his awareness, the
shadow may be either *primary or *secondary. As far as
the city is concerned, the shadow is secondary since
power, jealousy, laziness and *altered states of consciousness refer to tendencies not identified with.

Sociopath
An individual who breaks the stated rules of a given
society over a long period of time to the extent that he
constantly requires supervision or social control (such as
in a prison).

State
A *process in a static condition. Thus, the *primary
process is normally a state since it remains stable in spite
of strong changes in the world around and impinging
signals from *secondary processes within. A secondary
process implicit in a *complex or *illness can also be a
state. *Schizophrenia, bipolar disorders, and other mental
illnesses are states.

Synchronicity
A term defined by Jung, used here to mean a *secondary
process occurring in the world *channel.

Tardive dyskinesia (TD)
An iatrogenic disease characterized by movements which
are involuntary and purposeful. First evidence is often
masticatory-like movements of the surface of the tongue
or floor of the mouth. Occurs particularly in older
patients. TD can progress to neck, fingers, toes and face.
Postural control is also disturbed.

Unconscious

All *primary and *secondary processes which are not available to the observer's or experiencer's awareness.

BIBLIOGRAPHY

Abend, S., M. Porder and M. Willick, *Borderline Patients: Psychoanalytic Perspective*, New York, International University Press, 1983.

Adler, David, 'The Medical Model and Psychiatry's Tasks,' *Hospital and Community Psychiatry*, vol. 32, June 6 1981, p. 387.

American Psychiatric Association, *The Diagnostic and Statistical Manual of Mental Disorders* (DSM III), Washington, American Psychiatric Association, 1973.

Bassuk, E.L. and S. Gerson 'Deinstitutionalization and Mental Health Services,' *Sci. American*, vol. 238, 1978, pp. 46–53.

Bernheim, K.F., R.R.J. Lewine and Beale C.T., *The Caring Family: Living with Chronic Mental Illness*, New York, Random House, 1982.

Blanck, B., and R. Blanck, *Ego Psychology, II. Psychoanalytic Developmental Psychology*, New York, Columbia University Press, 1979.

Bleuler, E., *Dementia Praecox or the Group of Schizophrenias*, New York, International Universities Press, 1950.

Boyle, Joan and James Morriss, 'The Crisis in Medicine. Models, Myths and Metaphors, in *Et Cetera*, vol. 36, no. 3, 1979, pp. 261–74.

Chaiklin, Harris, Ed. *Marion Chace: Her Papers*. American Dance Therapy Assoc., 1975.

Clement-Jones, Vicky, 'The Role of the Endorphins in Neurology,' March 1983, vol. 227, p. 487.

Clifford, T., *Tibetan Buddist Medicine and Psychiatry*, Wellingborough: Aquarian Press, 1984.

Companion to Psychiatric Studies, 3rd ed. R. E. Kendell and A.K. Zealley (eds), Edinburgh, Churchill Livingstone, 1983.

Crombach, G., Psychopathologie aus der Sicht Veränderter Bewusstseinszustände, *Confinia Psychiatr.* 17, 1974, pp. 184–191.

Diagnostic and Statistical Manual of Mental Disorders (DSM III) (See The American Psychiatric Association)

Diamond, Ronald, 'Drugs and the Quality of Life: The Patient's Point of View, *J. Clin. Psychiatry* vol. no. 46, 5, (Sec. 2, May 1985.

Engel, George, 'The Need for a New Medical Model: A Challenge for Biomedicine,' *Science*, vol. 96, 8 April 1977, p. 129.

Freedman, Alfred, Harold Kaplan and Benjamin Sadock, *Modern Synopsis of Psychiatry/4*, Baltimore, Williams 4 Wilkins Co., 1984.

Freud, Sigmund, 'Psychoanalytic Notes Upon An Autobiographical Account of A Case of Paranoia, (Dementia Pradnoides),' *Collected Papers*, vol. 3., p. 316, London, The Hogarth Press and the Institute of Psychoanalysis, 1950.

Greist, J., J. Jefferson and R. Spitzer (ed), *Treatment of Mental Disorders*, New York, Oxford University Press, 1982.

Grey, Grady, Bainbridge Island, Washington, *Introduction to Process Oriented Psychology*, a film in three parts, 1987.

Henderson, D.K. and Gilespie, R.D., *Textbook of Psychiatry for Students and Practitioners*, tenth ed., revised by Ivor R.C. Batchelor, New York, Oxford University Press, 1969.

Introduction to Psychopharmacology, A Scope Publication, 1980, p. 58.

Johnson, D.A.W., et al., 'Antipsychotic Medication, Clinical Guidelines for Maintenance Therapy,' *J. Clin. Psychiatry*, vol. 46, no. 5, sec. 2, May 1985, pp. 6–15.

Jung, C.G., *The Psychogenesis of Mental Disease*, vol. 2, C.W., London, Routledge & Kegan Paul, 1974.

Kandel, Eric R., 'From Metapsychology to Molecular Biology: Explorations into the Nature of Anxiety,' *Am. J. Psychi.*, 140, 1983, pp. 127–93.

Karon, Berthran P. and Gary Vandenbos, *Psychotherapy of Schizophrenia, the Treatment of Choice*, New York, Jason Aronson, 1981.

Kessler, K. and J. Waletzky, 'Clinical Uses of Antipsychotics,' *Am. J. Psychi.*, vol. 138, no. 2, February 1981, pp. 202–9.

Kiev, Ari, *Transcultural Psychiatry*, New York, The Free Press, 1973.

Kohut, H., *The Restoration of Self*, New York, International Universities Press, 1977.

Kuhn, T., *The Structure of Scientific Revolutions*, Chicago, Ill., University of Chicago Press, 1970.

Lader, Malcolm, *Introduction to Psychopharmacology*, Kalamzoo, Mich., The Upjohn Company, 1980.

Laing, R.D., *The Politics of Experience*, New York, Ballantine Books, 1967.

Leary, Thomas, 'The Religious Experience: Its Production and Interpretation,' *Psychedelic Rev.*, 1, pp. 324–46.

Lehman, A.F., 'The Well Being of Chronic Mental Patients: Assessing their Quality of Life,' *Arch. Gen. Psychiatry*, 40, pp. 369–73, 1983.

Marmor, Judy, 'Systems Thinking in Psychiatry: Some Theoretical and Clinical Implications,' *Am. J. Psychi*, 140, pp. 833–38, 1983.

McGeer, P.L., J.C. Eccles and E.G. McGeer, *Molecular Neurobiology of the Mammalian Brain*, New York, Plenum, 1978.

Mindell, Arnold, *The Dreambody*, Boston, Sigo Press, 1982.

—— *Working with the Dreaming Body*, Routledge & Kegan Paul, Boston, 1985,

—— *River's Way*, Boston, Routledge & Kegan Paul, 1985.

—— *The Dreambody in Relationships*, Boston, Routledge & Kegan Paul, 1987.

—— *Inner Dreambodywork, Process Oriented Medication*, forthcoming.

Moline, Roland Sant Singh, Alan Morris and Herbert Meltzer, 'Family Expressed Emotion and Relapse in Schizophrenia,' *Am. J. Psychi.*, no. 142; no. 9, September 1985.

Perry, J.W., *The Far Side of Madness*, Englewood Cliffs, Prentice Hall, 1974.

Pribram, K., *Language of the Brain*, Englewood Cliffs, NJ, Prentice Hall, 1971.

—— 'Non Locality and Localization: A Review of the Place of the Holographic Hypothesis of Brain Function in Perception and Memory,' Preprint for the Tenth ICUS, November 1981.

Schoop, Trudi, and Peggy Mitchell, *Won't You Join the Dance? A Dancer's Essay into the Treatment of Psychosis*, Palo Alto, Ca., Mayfield Publishing Co., 1974.

—— *Masque of Madness*, Palo Alto, Ca., National Press, 1973.

Schweizerische Aerzte Zeitung, Bond 66, Heft 34, August, 1985.

Serafetinides, E.A., 'Cerebral Lateralization Research; From Speech and Epilepsy to Consciousness and Schizophrenia, *Psychiatric Annals*, vol. 15, no. 7, July 1985. pp. 427–429.

—— 'Cerebral Lateralizaation and Psychiatric Disorders: Introduction,' *Psychiatric Annals*, vol. 15. no. 7, July 1985. p. 423–427.

Smith, Andrew C., *Schizophrenia and Madness*, London Allen & Unwin, 1982.

Suzuki, Shunryu, *Zen Mind, Beginner's Mind*, New York, Weatherhill, 1976.

Szymanski, Herman, J. Simon and N. Gutterman *Am. J. Psychi.* March 83, p. 335.

Talbott, J.A. (ed.), *The Chronic Mentally Ill: Treatment Programs, Systems*, New York, Human Sciences Press, 1981.

Tart, Charles T., *States of Consciousness* El Cerito, Ca., Psychological Processes, 1975.

—— Altered States of Consciousness and the Search for Enlightenment, *Open Mind*, vol. 2, no. 4 January 1985.

Taylor, R.L. *Mind or Body: Distinguishing Psychological from Organic Disorders*, New York, McGraw Hill, 1982.

Torrey, E. Fuller, *Surviving Schizophrenia, A Family Manual*, New York, Harper & Row, 1983.

—— *The Death of Psychiatry*, Randor, Penn., Chilton, 1974.

Vaughn, C.E., M.A. Snyder and M.B. Jones, Family Factors in Schizophrenia Relapse: A California Replication of the British

Research on Expressed Emotion. *Schizophr. Bull.*, 8, pp. 425–6, 1982.

Weil, Andrew, *The Natural Mind*, London, Jonathan Cape, 1972.

Wilbur, Ken, 'The Development Spectrum and Psychopathology: Part I, States and Types of Pathology,' *J. of Transpers. Psych.* vol. 16, 1984, p. 75.

—— Part II, *J. of Transpers, Psych*, vol. 16, no. 2, 1984, p. 137.

INDEX

accidents, 73, 123, 128, 139, 141
active imagination, 26
acute episodes, 28, 52, 57, 104, 130
addiction, 111, 128–9, 138, 167;
  definition of, 111, 173; heroin, 4,
  13, 18, 74, 111–20
Adler, David, 8
affects, 3, 75, 155; definition of, 173;
  as inappropriate, 35, 38, 39
Africa, 55
aging, 95, 96
aggression, 23, 36, 44, 63, 70, 96,
  105, 113, 114, 153, 154, 155, 167,
  172; in neo-Reichian theory, 26–7
alchemy, 27
alcohol, 111, 121–33,, 138, 142–3,
  147, 159, 162
alcoholic, 138, 139, 158–9, 161, 169,
  170; couples, 123, 129, 137;
  definition of, 122; holographic
  aspects of, 129; primary process
  of, 124, 126, 130; secondary
  process of, 124, 126–7, 129–30, 132;
  and sober state, 129–30, 131, 132;
  state, 121–2, 123, 124, 125, 129–30,
  132
Alcoholics Anonymous, 132
alcoholism, 4, 13, 30, 73, 74, 114;
  definition of, 173; facts about, 121;
  and the collective, 121; meaning
  of, 132; process structure of,
  124–5, 129–30, 132; and
  sociopathy, 137
altered states, 5, 25, 74, 164, 172;
  accessing of, 121–2, 165; and
  channel blocking, 62, 64; and

channel switching, 62, 63, 64,
  164; and creativity, 64; definition
  of, 173; and drugs, 59, 112, 117–18;
  and hypnotic processes, 61; and
  illness, 62; and metacommunication, 64; process
  structure of, 129–30; working
  with, 84, 164–5
American Psychiatric Association's
  Manual on Mental Disorders, 137,
  149
amphetamines, 111
amplification, 79; of body
  symptoms, 24; of channel
  phenomena, 76–7; of criticism,
  128; of proprioception, 81; as a
  symptom, 77; of verbal statement,
  120
analytical psychology, 11, 39;
  paradigm in, 26, 40, 163–4; and
  role of analyst, 163–4
anger, 37, 88–9, 117, 119, 131, 140,
  153, 155, 156, 158–60, 164
Anthropos theory, 41–2
antipsychiatry, 8, 15–16
antisocial disorders, 16
anxiety attacks, 164–5
appendectomies, 78
appetite, 93
archetypes, as collective, 39, 171;
  definition of, 174; experiences of,
  8, 14; and symptoms, 22
asana, 81
aspirin, 22, 122
Atman experience, 15
atoms, 100